T0266951

"The progressive Christian movement asks us to 'reimagine' Jesus as one who wasn't the Son of God, wasn't born of a virgin, didn't do miracles, didn't rise from the dead, and isn't coming again. It insists, with unabashed narcissism, that Jesus needs to change to be more like us, rather than us changing to be more like him. *Hijacking Jesus* offers clarity, logic, and substantial biblical backing to show the way back to the timeless truths about Jesus found in Scripture."

  —**Jeff Myers**, PhD, president of Summit Ministries

"Over a hundred years ago, J. Gresham Machen argued that the liberal Christianity of that day was not merely a variation of the faith, but a different faith altogether. The heirs of that movement persist today, attempting to redefine who Jesus has revealed Himself to be. As John Stott said, 'Christianity is Christ.' To redefine Him is to invent a different faith. In *Hijacking Jesus*, Jason Jimenez brings a much-needed clarity to who Jesus is, how He is misrepresented in progressive Christianity, and what's at stake."

  —**John Stonestreet,** president of the Colson Center, host of
  BreakPoint

"The Apostle Paul warns that some 'will be led astray' by those who proclaim 'another Jesus' (2 Cor. 11:3–4). That's why we need *Hijacking Jesus*! Jason Jimenez exposes how progressive Christianity professes a counterfeit Christ rather than the real Jesus revealed in Scripture. As Jimenez puts it: they're hijacking Jesus. Using an easy-to-follow comparative approach, Jimenez helps us both understand the problems with the progressive Jesus and see the uniqueness of the historical Jesus. At a time when some people are confused about who Jesus is, this book brings much-needed clarity."

  —**Tim Barnett**, apologist, Red Pen Logic with Mr. B, coauthor
  of *The Deconstruction of Christianity*

Hijacking Jesus

Hijacking

Jesus

How Progressive Christians Are Remaking Him and Taking Over His Church

JASON JIMENEZ

SALEM
BOOKS

an imprint of Regnery Publishing
Washington, D.C.

Salem Books™ is a trademark of Salem Communications Holding Corporation. Regnery® and its colophon are registered trademarks of Salem Communications Holding Corporation.
Cataloging-in-Publication data on file with the Library of Congress.

ISBN: 978-1-68451-408-3
eISBN: 978-1-68451-470-0

Published in association with The Bindery Agency: www.TheBinderyAgency.com.

Published in the United States by
Salem Books
An Imprint of Regnery Publishing
A Division of Salem Media Group
Washington, D.C.
www.SalemBooks.com

Manufactured in the United States of America

10 9 8 7 6 5 4 3 2 1

Books are available in quantity for promotional or premium use. For information on discounts and terms, please visit our website: www.SalemBooks.com.

For those faithful worshipers of Jesus who confess Him as the King of kings and the Lord of lords (Revelation 19:16)

CONTENTS

PART 3

Three Reinvented Images of Jesus — 163

Author's Note

While writing this book, I delivered several lectures to live audiences on some of the material. I wanted to see how audiences would respond and was curious to learn directly from people with real-life experiences with progressive Christianity. What I discovered along the way shocked me to the core.

I was stunned by the number of people I came across who had deconverted from biblical faith to progressive Christianity or were altogether confused about the worldview. Never in my life have I felt so compelled to write a book as I do now.

I wrote *Hijacking Jesus* to help biblical Christians defend their faith while making a convincing case for those who might be falling for the elusiveness of progressive Christianity to change course. Perhaps you are currently disenchanted with evangelical Christianity and find yourself leaning more toward a progressive point of view on a few biblical and moral issues—but you wouldn't call yourself a progressive Christian. Wherever you find yourself, this book is for you!

One thing that became clear as I wrote is how the term "progressive Christianity" never seems to mean the same thing among progressive Christians. This confused me, as I am attempting to articulate progressive Christianity and its "beliefs" respectfully and soundly. This is why I felt it important to bring in as many progressive Christian voices as possible—so readers can see for themselves what they are actually teaching. Although my main objective is to unravel the controversial narrative of Jesus painted by progressive Christians, I also want to introduce readers to the broad spectrum of views held by progressive Christians who represent different fields and positions of influence. Their perspectives not only uproot the fabric of historic Christianity but overhaul the very identity and integrity of Jesus and push the boundaries of biblical theology.

This is an investigative and scholastic work that addresses perennial questions about the nature and doctrine of Jesus, seeking to uncover His true identity based on the context in which He lived. It tests the progressive Christian view of Him while defending the four canonical gospels (Matthew, Mark, Luke, and John) as the most credible sources for the facts of Jesus's life, teachings, miracles, death, and resurrection. It will teach you to corroborate the historical data of Jesus, examine the theological doctrines presented in the narration of church history, and attest to the experiential and spiritual vitality that comes with believing that Jesus Christ is Lord and Savior.

Thank you for choosing to read this book.

Jason Jimenez

Introduction

What comes to mind when you hear the word "hijacking"?

Most people think of things like the four airplanes that Islamic terrorists seized and flew into American buildings on 9/11—one of the darkest days in American history that permanently changed how we fly the friendly skies.

It's mind-blowing to realize terrorists exploited lax airport security for years because airlines feared slowing the process and frustrating their passengers. So they did nothing.

Until 9/11.

In the days and weeks after that grim apex, airports finally ramped up their security to prevent hijackings and ensure flight safety for passengers. As a result, hijackings became increasingly rare. Today, the odds of your flight being hijacked are 10,408,947 to 1. Therefore, it's safe to assume most people reading this book have never been on a hijacked plane.

The Standoff

But there's another form of hijacking that has far more eternal consequences: the attempt to hijack Jesus.

Over the last several decades, progressive Christian leaders have been theologically and spiritually motivated to seize Jesus as resurrected Savior and radically reinterpret Him as a Jewish mystic or as a manifestation of God devoid of divine claims and miracles.

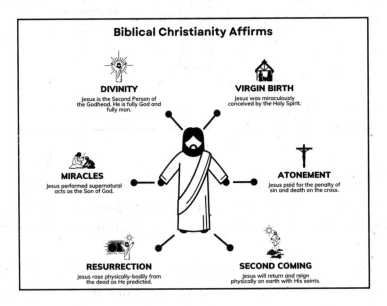

Biblical Christianity solidly asserts all these things based on the Word of God. But in the postmodern era, the call of progressive Christian voices "remaking Jesus" is becoming more tantalizing to many.

Progressive Christians say their "modernizing of Jesus" makes Him a more friendly and accepting figure for self-identified Christians. They say they are simply "refreshing" Jesus (sort of like Subway keeps refreshing its sandwiches).

However, what progressive Christianity actually does is reject the historical and biblical narrative of Jesus Christ.

Therefore, it is unmistakably apparent that progressive Christianity isn't simply "making adjustments" to Jesus's image. It's far worse: They are outright hijacking Jesus. And they are not subtle about it.

That may be startling to hear, but it's worth pointing out that progressive Christians don't see their version of Jesus as a hijacking. They see it as a recovery—a rescuing of Jesus from the dogmatic rigidity of traditional Christianity.[1]

As a matter of fact, progressive teachers believe the original hijackers of Jesus belonged to the Pauline movement. They argue that Christian traditionalists were unrelenting in their assault on Jesus and suppressed His inclusive teachings—and eventually divinized Him, like a sort of Greek god.

In his classic book, *Jesus: Uncovering the Life, Teachings, and Relevance of a Spiritual Revolutionary*, the late theologian Marcus J. Borg claims that through the centuries, pagan worshipers formulated various doctrines that eventually morphed the image of Jesus into that of a divine Savior.[2]

However, despite what progressive Christians want people to believe, their portrayal of Jesus carries significant historical, theological, and spiritual implications, according to the Bible.

Biblical Christians contend that the portrait of Jesus progressive scholars have configured is nowhere to be found in the capsules of history or the Gospel accounts. They are caricatures concocted from revisionist theories of church history, framed by the ideological perspective of liberal intellectualism.

In this "modernized" version of Christianity, progressive Christians deceptively challenge Protestant churches with their conventional belief of Jesus as more of a "liberator" than a "Savior," and contend that they bring enlightenment to the disconcerted minds of Christians, creating a standoff over the true identity of Jesus.

But you know what?

The Church has only become susceptible to these attacks through its own laxity in preserving doctrinal truth. We have grown deficient in the rigorous and passionate defense of the historic Christian faith.

As a result, it is now far easier for progressive theological hijackers to seize the identity of Jesus, and a big reason why we are seeing such a high number of deconversions today.

Countermeasures

Yet, despite these formidable attacks, I believe many Christians, including you, are eager to learn and ready to take back the truth of Jesus—revealed and exalted as the Son of God in the New Testament.

Just as the aviation industry enhanced security efforts after 9/11, Christians need to put a new defense strategy in place to counter the theological hijackings of progressive Christians. Sometimes doctrinal debates (not acrimonious disputes) and divisions are fitting, even healthy, for the Church to experience. It forces Christians to pay closer attention to the teachings around them and learn to stand up for their beliefs. We must be more like the Berean Jews, who "searched the Scriptures daily" (Acts 17:11) to ensure that what they were taught aligned with the Word of God.

Uncovering the Truth

Out of all the doctrinal debates and religious conversations in the world, the ultimate question is this: Who is Jesus Christ? For that reason, allow me to briefly explain the flow of the book.

Part One explores the roots of progressive Christianity and reveals major conspiracies through church history, as well as where the progressive version currently stands in today's church based on key players and beliefs.

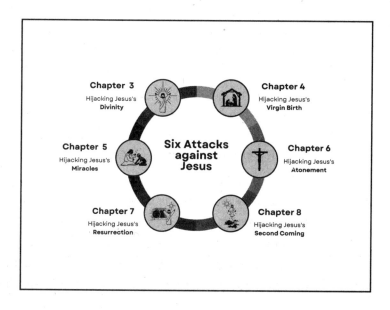

Part Two presents side-by-side comparisons of progressive Christianity with biblical Christianity, strengthening your knowledge of the two opposing worldviews and giving you the necessary tools to counter progressive Christianity.

Part Three examines the three most popular "versions" of Jesus progressive Christians advocate: Jesus, the Jewish Mystic; Jesus, the Woke Teacher; and Jesus, the Revolutionist.

Image credit: Amy Jimenez and Supersienar

Following each false narrative of Jesus are helpful takeaways you can use when talking with progressive Christians.

Throughout this book, I will use the term "biblical Christianity" as the standard of historic orthodoxy most consistent with Scripture (the infallible Word of God) and whose doctrinal truths of God, Jesus, man, and salvation are faithfully preserved and theologically articulated in the Apostles' Creed, Nicene Creed, and Athanasian Creed.[3]

Hijacking Jesus is a faith-cultivating book that passionately invites Christians to come face-to-face with the unadulterated truth of Jesus

Christ through the richness of history and the illumination of the holy Scriptures.

I realize some people will pick up this book and immediately think I am out to get progressive Christians. I hope you believe me when I say that is not the case. My heart is not to criticize them but to critique their worldview in its proper context and warn of the dire consequences of falsely portraying Jesus.

I invite you to journey with me as we uncover the nucleus of Jesus's ministry on Earth and pray that you capture His eternal beauty and splendor in your life.

PART 1

THE CONSPIRATORIAL RISE OF PROGRESSIVE CHRISTIANITY

How did progressive Christianity come onto the theological scene? What do progressive Christians stand for? Part 1 answers those two primary questions by surveying many critical historical moments that shaped liberal theology, touching on prominent liberal scholars who paved the way to the progressive Christian worldview in varied disciplines through the last several centuries.

CHAPTER 1

The Conspiracy to
Hijack Jesus

"After nearly twenty-five years of pastoral ministry, I was encountering Jesus in new ways that posed profound challenges to many of the assumptions I had grown comfortable with," writes Brian Zahnd. He seeks to remove what he calls "the layers of lacquer comprised of the cultural assumptions" that prevent us from encountering Jesus.[1]

That sounds very nice. But Zahnd is really saying that he has discovered a new way to look at Jesus that is not bogged down by tradition and doctrine. That's the same message other progressive Jesus activists share: that their contemporary scholarship has broken away from the religious encrustations of the ages, allowing them to uncover Jesus through a reappraisal process that points to a "new" and "fresh" perspective of Him that is not restrained by dogma or tradition.

Moreover, they question biblical Christians, insinuating they've gotten Jesus all wrong.

In his book *The Secret Message of Jesus*, Brian McLaren, founder of Cedar Ridge Community Church in Spencerville, Maryland, asks, "What if we have developed a religion that makes reverent and honoring statements about Jesus but doesn't teach what Jesus taught in the manner he taught it?"[2]

Progressive Christians want to revise Christian history and reduce the gospel narratives to *kerygma* (not historical) accounts to float exotic storylines that supersede the original intent and meaning of the four canonical gospels: Matthew, Mark, Luke, and John.

Progressive Christians boast that

- their newfound knowledge of Jesus is more profound than the Bible and contains richer insights, metaphors, and meaning that will awaken Christians like never before, and
- their Christianity is more contemporary and inclusive—not oppressive, like dull, traditional Christianity.

Legendary writer Peter Enns, who teaches on the Old and New Testaments at Eastern University, reasons that "progressive Christianity" should not be a pejorative term, but rather a phrase that indicates inquisitive faith that evolves with the ever-changing truth of the Scripture[3]—as if to say, according to David Gushee, that progressive Christians have done the faith a favor by cutting it loose from the constraints of fundamentalist orthodoxies.[4]

In laying out the various modifications of Jesus throughout the past several hundred years, we must start by examining four heretical movements that sprang into action early on.

Gnosticism (a Form of Docetism)

In the late first century, Marcion[5] began a movement known as *Gnosticism*, which taught that Christ appeared to be a man but was not *fully* human. He taught that there was no connection between the Old Testament and the New Testament, between the God of the Jews and the God of the Christians.

The Gnostic movement is dualistic. It holds to a Platonic system that claims everything made of matter (physical elements) is evil and corrupt; thus, only spiritual elements are considered pure.

Considering matter to be evil, Docetism denies that Jesus took on a human body, holding that He was more a phantom figure than a real human being. Therefore, Jesus's body, death, and resurrection are merely illusions.

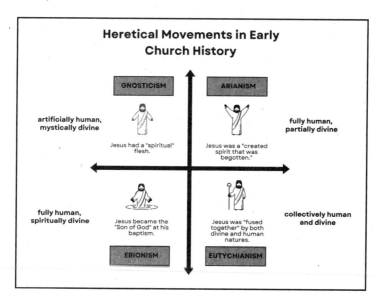

Heretical Movements in Early Church History

GNOSTICISM — artificially human, mystically divine — Jesus had a "spiritual" flesh.

ARIANISM — fully human, partially divine — Jesus was a "created spirit that was begotten."

EBIONISM — fully human, spiritually divine — Jesus became the "Son of God" at his baptism.

EUTYCHIANISM — collectively human and divine — Jesus was "fused together" by both divine and human natures.

Ebionism

In the second century, Ebionism taught that Jesus was not God—only a man who decided to become the "Son of God" at his baptism.

Ebionites fell into two categories: The first viewed Jesus as nothing more than a great moral teacher with extraordinary abilities some believed to be supernatural; the second believed Jesus's birth was supernatural but did not lend credence to the idea that He first existed in Heaven as part of the Triune Godhead before His virgin birth.

Arianism

In the fourth century, Arius, a Libyan priest, wrote that Jesus was not of the same essence or nature of God. He reasoned that since Jesus was "begotten" (God's created spirit), He could not be eternal. Thus, for Arius, Jesus possessed something similar to God's deity but was not equal to God.

"The net result of this teaching," writes author J. N. D. Kelly, "was to reduce the Son to a demigod."[6] In 325, the Council of Nicea produced a creed saying that Jesus Christ was "of one substance with the Father" and "was made man" to combat Arius's dissenting view that Jesus was not fully God.

Eutychianism

Eutyches of Constantinople taught that Jesus Christ had one nature only. His body was fused by both divine and human natures, which made each partial fulfillments of one another.

Infancy Gospels
(2nd–4th Centuries)

As various views of Jesus's humanity and divinity circulated among the early Church, a few infancy gospels offering stories of His childhood came on the scene. This small group of documents served more to entertain than to promote a sectarian Savior.

The authors of *Reinventing Jesus: How Contemporary Skeptics Miss the Real Jesus and Mislead Popular Culture* report what they included:

> The earliest infancy gospels are the Protevangelium of James (more a story of Mary) and the Infancy Gospel of Thomas (not the same Gospel of Thomas). Most scholars date these books to the second half of the second century. Some later infancy gospels are based on these first two, including the Gospel of Pseudo-Matthew, the Arabic Infancy Gospel, Arundel 404, and the History of Joseph the Carpenter.[7]

However, as much as progressive Christians argue that the Infancy Gospels are authentic stories of Jesus's life, historic orthodox Christianity rejects them because they promote Docetism, are centuries removed from the canonical gospels, and have no historical or theological connection to the canonical gospels. Moreover, the Patristic Fathers—the pastors and theologians who lived between the end of the apostolic age to medieval times—dismissed them for their mythical views of Jesus.

Rationalism and Enlightenment (17th–18th Centuries)

During this time, a philosophical and scientific revolution grew and began challenging faith and religious establishments. The Bible could no longer be considered a trusted document because its "miracle stories" contradicted science. As a result, Christianity (and religion in general) became subjective, personal, and a pragmatic means to form morals and values in life.

The **Enlightenment Period** ultimately rejected supernaturalism and promoted two streams of thought: (1) **Unitarianism** (which rejects the Trinity and Jesus's divinity) and (2) **Deism** (a religious framework that denies God's involvement in the world, the divinity of Christ, miracles, and the divine inspiration of the Bible).

The **Racovian Catechism (1605)** was a religious document published in Poland by the Socinians, a group with ties to Unitarianism that came out of Arianism. The Catechism reads, "Since [Jesus] has necessarily a human nature, he could not be God, nor, indeed, have existed antecedently to his birth."[8] The Catechism affirms that the Father is the one and only true God, Jesus is fully human (not God), and the Holy Spirit is the power of the Father. The Catechism also laid out extensive reasoning for rejecting the vicarious atonement of Jesus Christ and held that human beings could each work out their own path of forgiveness with God.

Benedict Spinoza (1632–1677) taught that theology was not science. Thus, Scripture had to be subjected to reason and interpreted through rationalism. Much of modern liberalism springs from Spinoza's efforts to desupernaturalize the Bible and secularize religion.

Richard Simon ("Father of Modern Biblical Criticism," 1638–1712) was one of the first people to attack the Bible, stating in *Critical History of the Text of the New Testament* that it is full of contradictions.

François-Marie Arouet ("Voltaire," 1694–1778) was a French philosopher and deist who embraced an antisupernatural perspective of the Bible: He believed Jesus was close to being a spiritual genius, but short of being God. Voltaire was not in the business of reforming Christianity in France, but given the sectarian corruption between the Church and the government, he aimed to free the people from not only totalitarianism but from believing in the core tenets of Christianity as well.

David Hume ("The Father of Skepticism," 1711–1776), in his *Enquiry Concerning Human Understanding*, stated that all meaningful ideas are either actual by definition or must be determined by sensory experience. Hume also said that any statement that is not mathematically related to itself and not empirically or factually verifiable is meaningless. According to Hume, the Bible does not meet these standards and, therefore, is false.

Immanuel Kant ("The Father of Agnosticism," 1724–1804) dehistoricized Adam, rejected the teaching of original sin, classified Jesus as the archetype of moral goodness, and argued that, therefore, there is no need for atonement because each person must work out their own wrongs and attempt to make them right.

Romanticism to Realism
(18th–19th Centuries)

Romanticism was a literary movement of deep artistic emotion and expression of the sublime that reshaped specific theological terms and meanings. Realism, on the other hand, focused on objective reality and sought to refute many of the Romanticists' groundless claims.

In due course, naturalism became the overarching worldview—introducing a naturalistic method by which to study the Bible and other historical writings.

George Wilhelm Friedrich Hegel (1770–1831) wrote two critical books that radically shifted people's view of Christianity in the nineteenth century: *Phenomenology of Spirit* and *Lectures on the Philosophy of Religion*. From Plotinus, Hegel embraced a form of pantheism (all is God). Later, Hegel came to see God and the world merging as One (i.e., panentheism—the divine intersecting through all spheres of creation while also extending past space and time). According to Hegel, God is not a transcendental Creator but is One in essence with the world. He interpreted the incarnation of Jesus in panentheistic terms: the infinite Spirit (i.e., God) meshed with the finite, causing Jesus to become the God-man (duality). As did many of his predecessors, Hegel desupernaturalized Jesus, interpreting His death and resurrection as nothing more than a Greek tragedy.

Friedrich Schleiermacher ("Father of Modern Liberalism," 1768–1834) was heavily influenced by Kant. His two monumental works attacking the credibility of the Bible, Jesus, and Christianity are *The Christian Faith* and *On Religion: Speeches to Its Cultured Despisers*. Schleiermacher argued that religion is a matter of feeling and that Jesus was the perfect example and manifestation of God-consciousness. That is, He reached the ideal embodiment of God's love and reproduced God's activity in the world. Schleiermacher attempted to merge ideas of the Enlightenment with Christian doctrines—which fundamentally altered their meaning and fidelity to the Bible.[9]

Søren Kierkegaard ("The Father of Existentialism," 1813–1855) taught that there is no essential truth and that faith and history oppose one another. Kierkegaard believed that what little is known of Jesus and His divinity is based not on historical facts but solely on faith (which is personal and subjective). Though you cannot trust the Bible as a reliable source, he surmised, you can still embrace its spiritual teachings and values.

The First (Old) Quest (1778–1906): Endeavoring to Be Historical

The purpose of the "Jesus Quests" was to paint an accurate portrait of Jesus of Nazareth. To do this, many modern Jesus scholars felt it necessary to separate the facts of the "historical Jesus" from those of the "biblical Jesus."

It is correct to say that these quests take over the historic, orthodox view of Jesus Christ to reimagine Him through the sociocultural lens of progressive scholarship.

Of the significance of the First Quest, Dr. Gregory Boyd, senior pastor of Woodland Hills Church in St. Paul, Minnesota, writes,

> These scholars accepted as historical basic features of Mark's Gospel but rejected, or at least radically reinterpreted, both the supernatural features of Jesus' ministry and the New Testament's portrayal of him as divine. The only Jesus that could be relevant for faith in the modern age, they believed, was one who was freed from the mythological trappings of his first-century world.[10]

This release of the "mythological trappings" of Jesus was observed by several liberal scholars (primarily German) listed below.

Hermann Reimarus (1694–1768), a German philosopher who wrote an explosive essay entitled "The Aims of Jesus and His Disciples." This was the first history of the criticism that undermined traditional scholarship by disavowing the credibility of biblical miracles and the idea that the prophets and disciples received divine revelation from God.[11]

David Friedrich Strauss (1808–1874), a German liberal Protestant who published the acclaimed book, *The Life of Jesus, Critically Examined* (1835–1836). Strauss put forth two alternatives when examining the life of Jesus: supernaturalism vs. rationalism. Strauss believed Jesus regarded Himself as the Messiah, but most of the contents of the biblical gospels are false. In essence, Strauss holds that Jesus was a mythical character and the gospel accounts (anonymous documents written late in the second century) were forged from myths and creative storytelling.

Ernst Troeltsch (1865–1923), a German Protestant theologian and foremost spokesperson of liberal Protestantism. In his 1898 essay, "On Historical and Dogmatic Method in Theology," he challenges how historical criticism was conducted before the twentieth century.

Horace Bushnell (1802–1876), an American Congregational minister, liberal theologian, and mystic, is considered one of the founders of modern Protestantism and a prominent voice for "progressive orthodoxy."

Albrecht Ritschl (1822–1889), a German Lutheran theologian and a contemporary of Schleiermacher who took a Kantian approach to reconstructing theology. Ritschl criticized the doctrine of original sin, questioned the legitimacy of historical facts of Jesus, and denounced salvation through Jesus Christ. For Ritschl, advancing the Kingdom of God is to live by the moral teachings of Jesus.

William Wrede (1859–1906), a German scholar and Lutheran theologian who published *The Messianic Secret* in 1901. Wrede strongly believed that the gospel accounts falsely portrayed Jesus. He emphasized that the Book of Mark, the first recorded gospel, is not historically credible because the writer was motivated by theological interests.

The "No Quest" Period (1907–1953): The Church Crafted a Savior

The final analysis from this period of scholarship produced a minimalistic profile of Jesus and His surroundings, resulting in skepticism and a move in academic circles to deem Jesus inconsequential.

Albert Schweitzer (1875–1965), a German theologian and philosopher who wrote *The Quest of the Historical Jesus: A Critical Study of Its Progress from Reimarus to Wrede* (1906). In it, Schweitzer pulls from Johannes Weiss's previous work (1892) which portrayed Jesus as a misguided apocalyptic prophet who strongly believed in the world's coming doom. In *The Mystery of the Kingdom of God*, Schweitzer argued that at His baptism, Jesus believed Himself to be the Messiah, but in the end, He was nothing more than an enigma.

Rudolf Bultmann (1884–1976), a famous German New Testament professor and Lutheran theologian who wrote *New Testament and Mythology* (1941). This landmark book advanced the antisupernatural presupposition first advocated by Spinoza and Hume onto the Bible. Bultmann believed the only way to interpret the Bible was through a mythological framework. Much of his "demythologization" was an effort to weaken neoorthodox methods of interpretation. In the end, for Bultmann, Jesus was a misguided hero who never ushered in His Kingdom before He died.

Paul Tillich (1886–1965), a German-American existentialist philosopher and Lutheran theologian who published a three-volume work called *Systematic Theology*, which seldom quotes the Scripture. For Tillich, the biblical stories carried symbolic truth and meaning but treated Jesus's incarnation as more existential than literal and much of His history as uncertain.[12]

Adolf von Harnack (1851–1930), a Baltic German Lutheran theologian who viewed Jesus not as the Son of God, but as a liberal religious reformer who reached serenity. In *What is Christianity?* (1901), Harnack utilizes his historical-critical method to interpret the Bible, surmising that the doctrines of the Trinity, the virgin birth, and the Incarnation were nothing more than concepts derived from Greek thought.[13]

Karl Barth (1886–1968) was a prolific writer and one of the premier neoorthodox theologians who rejected natural theology, the infallibility of the Bible, and advocated universalism (the idea that all people will be saved, no matter what). In *Church Dogmatics*, Barth wrote that it is difficult to get historical information about Jesus Christ.

The Second Quest (1954–1988):
A Furtherance of Historical Skepticism

The Second Quest—a less radical approach to the person of Jesus—endeavored to return to a traditional form of criticism (analysis of the Bible) by focusing on the reliance and relevance of ancient documents, avoiding Bultmann's overtones and exaggerations. However, the "Historical Jesus" does not necessarily support the Jesus of Nazareth depicted in the gospels.

Ernst Käsemann (1906–1998), a German scholar and Lutheran theologian who wrote *The Problem of the Historical Jesus*, sparking the Second Quest in the 1950s. Käsemann did not accept Christ as the Messiah, but at least embraced many of His ethical teachings.

Joachim Jeremias (1900–1979), a German Lutheran scholar, focused on the Aramaic teaching of Jesus to leverage the authenticity of His background. His book *The Parables of Jesus* (1947) sought to integrate Jesus's Jewishness and parabolical teachings with the traditions of Judaism.

James M. Robinson (1924–2016), in his landmark book *A New Quest of the Historical Jesus* (1959; revised in 1983), expressed the illegitimacy of the First Quest and argued that the only way to understand the gospels is to see them as writings of faith (*kerygma*) in the early Church that reveal Jesus's existential nature.

The Third Quest (1989–Present):
The Jewish Background Speaks to an Existential Jesus

The outcome of the Third Quest (also known as "The Renaissance of Jesus") was the belief that Jesus can be whatever you make Him out to be: eschatological prophet, Galilean holy man, Jewish sage, cynic, political insurrectionist, revolutionist, zealot, or peasant artisan.

The Third Quest argues that the Gospel of Mark (the first gospel written) gets its information from an early outside source known by contemporary scholars as "Q Source." The letter "Q" comes from the German word *quelle*, meaning "source." It is from this unknown source that the Gospel of Mark establishes the base for the historicity of Jesus. As such, it disputes Matthew, Luke, and John because they are so different and "not in harmony" with one another. Third Questers say there is little coherence and consistent teaching about Jesus that can be trusted because the evidence runs contrary to what written gospels say.[14]

Several scholars, including N. T. Wright, have attempted to rescue the Jesus of Christianity from liberal German scholarship. However, the Third Quest predominantly has remained grounded on a Spinozan interpretation of faith and reason—resulting in the gospels being treated as unreliable sources, along with casting doubt on the historicity of Jesus Christ.

George B. Caird (1917–1984), an English Congregationalist and theologian, authored *Jesus and the Jewish Nation* (1965), exploring Jesus's roots and identity in the nation of Israel. He surmised that: (1) The Christ of faith is different than the Jesus of history; (2) Christology has nothing to do with Jesus's Messiahship; and (3) the concepts of salvation and faith are to be rejected.

E. P. Sanders (1937–2022) was an American New Testament scholar who, in 1985, published *Jesus and Judaism*, remaking Jesus as a Jewish reformist. In 1993, Sanders wrote *The Historical Figure of Jesus*, denying His virgin birth, His miracles, and the idea that the canonical gospels should hold any real influence over Christianity.[15]

Robert Funk (1926–2005), a progressive New Testament scholar, was intensely skeptical of orthodox Christianity. In 1985, he founded the Jesus Seminar, a group of scholars who separate the "Jesus of history" from the "Christ of faith," accept less than 20 percent of the words of Jesus recorded in the canonical gospels, and repudiate the claims about His resurrection.

John Dominic Crossan (1934–), an Irish-American New Testament scholar and historian, is a prominent member of the Jesus Seminar. In one of his best-known books, *The Historical Jesus: The Life of a Mediterranean Jewish Peasant* (1991), Crossan champions the idea that Jesus was an illiterate Jewish peasant and magician who fought Roman imperialism, that His body was tossed aside and eaten by dogs after He was killed, and that His divinity and resurrection are simply "metaphors" that speak to the disciples' newfound faith after His death.

Marcus Borg (1942–2015) was an American New Testament scholar with an international reputation among liberal and progressive Christians. Borg interpreted Jesus in the context of Jewish apocalyptic themes. He embraced Jesus as a religious healer, a social prophet, a wise teacher, and the founder of the Christian movement, but nothing more.[16]

John Shelby Spong (1931–2021) was a bishop in the Episcopal Church. In his book *Jesus for the Non-Religious* (2008), Spong claims we do not know who His parents were, denies the claim that Jesus was born in Bethlehem to a virgin, and explains away the prophetic Scriptures as superstition.

Dale C. Allison (1955–) is an American New Testament scholar with liberal leanings who has contributed extensively to the research on the historical Jesus. In his prolific books, *The Historical Christ and the Theological Jesus* (2009) and *Constructing Jesus: Memory, Imagination, and History* (2010), Allison diminishes the historical credibility of the gospels and undercuts the apostles' defense of Jesus's divinity and literal physical resurrection.

Now that you have gotten a crash course on the history of hijacking Jesus, I will show you how progressive Christianity came about and piece together a few collective explanations that make up the worldview itself.

CHAPTER 2

New Theology on the Block

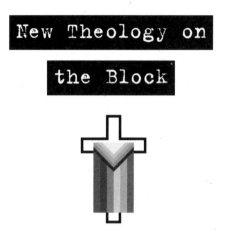

The Rise of Progressive Christianity

Over the last several decades, progressive Christianity has been rising. The more this worldview has materialized, the steadier its following has become.

As mentioned earlier, the Age of Enlightenment opened the door to reconceptualizing the fundamentals of historic Christianity.

After Rationalism and Romanticism, Darwinian evolution emerged in the nineteenth century and undercut Christianity by challenging the existence of God, creation *ex nihilo*, the supernatural, and the *imago Dei*. The dismissal of the supernatural only created more traction for secularism—which brought on a level of public scrutiny of the Bible never seen before. Biblical criticism became the accepted academic standard among universities—restructuring the way scholars, pastors, and theologians examine it and calling into question the divine claims of Jesus.

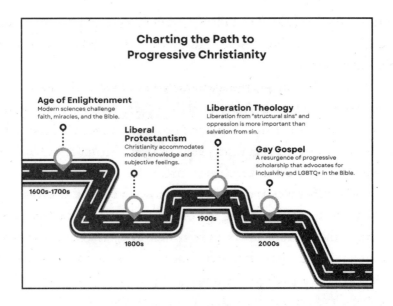

Charting the Path to Progressive Christianity

Age of Enlightenment
Modern sciences challenge faith, miracles, and the Bible.

Liberal Protestantism
Christianity accommodates modern knowledge and subjective feelings.

Liberation Theology
Liberation from "structural sins" and oppression is more important than salvation from sin.

Gay Gospel
A resurgence of progressive scholarship that advocates for inclusivity and LGBTQ+ in the Bible.

1600s-1700s

1800s

1900s

2000s

As confidence in modernity grew, Christian liberal theology stretched its tentacles into various conservative outlets and denominations. Liberal Protestantism sprang up, seeking a more scientific and inclusive mindset that elevates human experience and reason. This sect views Jesus as an exceptionally moral man whose teachings on liberation and morality are regarded as enduring truths that need to be observed to this day.

As a result, theological and cultural clashes between conservative and liberal Protestants turned into a bitter competition—resulting in many liberals seeking to establish "more inclusive" communities founded on their modified beliefs and values.

As liberal Protestants advanced a communal faith that fashioned their metrics of theology, attendance in mainline churches spiked nationwide. The steady growth of converts gave way to the Social Gospel and liberation theology blowing up in the mid-1900s—becoming fertile ground for the seeds of progressive Christianity. All the ingredients were there: Kierkegaard's existentialism mixed with Tillich's individualism and "oneness with God," with a double dose of Bultmann's demythologizing of the biblical narrative.

By the 1930s, neo-orthodoxy emerged from liberal theology and gained some traction in America in the 1940s and 1950s. Many contributors, such as Barth, Tillich, Emil Brunner, and Reinhold Niebuhr, deliberately rejected liberalism's view of God, the Bible, and sin, and attempted to correct its theological mistakes.

Many self-professing Christians traded in biblical doctrines for biblical social ethics, leading to debates and conflicts between conservative and liberal Christians who were sympathetic to socialism. By the 1960s, mainline denominations were flourishing and incorporating various aspects of the Social Gospel, liberation gospel, black theology, and progressive evangelical social ethics.

In the 1970s, Jim Wallis—arguably one of the leading standard bearers of progressive Christianity—launched *Sojourners*, a magazine that aided many progressive Christians in their faith views regarding social justice and sociopolitical issues.

By the 1990s, many modernists, moderates, and liberal Christians with postmodern leanings began to coalesce. The group would quickly self-identify as "progressive Christians."

In 1994, Episcopal priest James Adams founded the Center of Progressive Christianity. In 2010, the organization was renamed ProgressiveChristianity.org. Shortly afterward, ProgressiveChristianity.org partnered with liberal Christian theologian and retired Episcopal Bishop John Shelby Spong (1931–2021) to disseminate Spong's online work, ProgressingSpirit.com, and circulate his book, *A New Christianity for a New World*, as a pivotal piece of literature to advance progressive Christianity worldwide.

By the early 2000s, emergent leaders such as Tony Jones and Brian McLaren began to capture and publish content for theologically and politically liberal audiences. McLaren's books *A New Kind of Christian* (2001) and *A Generous Orthodoxy* (2004) are seen by many Christians as a manifesto of the emerging-church conversation and acted as roadmaps for many left-leaning evangelicals, Social Gospel advocates, and mainline Protestants.

Homosexuality became a key social and moral issue for this group, and they used it to change the conservative Christians' minds wherever possible. The "Gay Gospel" became a centerpiece of the movement, winning its ultimate victory when the U.S. Supreme Court overran states' rights to legalize same-sex marriage nationwide in 2015.

What's in a Name? Defining Progressive Christianity

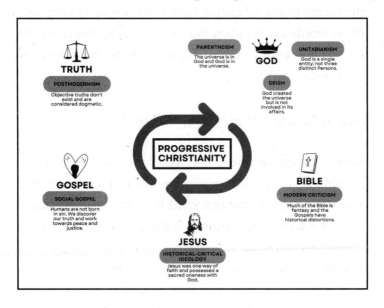

Progressive Christianity does not match orthodox Christianity's historical, traditional, and theological facts and beliefs in many ways.

Progressive Christianity, on some level, seeks to be "orthodox," but without the dogma, creeds, and literal rendering of the Bible as a supernatural book.

Progressive Christians do not consider their "reformulations" to be hijacking biblical Christianity. They see it as rescuing a dying religion.

But you don't have to take my word for it. Here are a few quotes taken directly from their books:

John Shelby Spong, *Why Christianity Must Change or Die*:

> To be called an orthodox Christian does not mean that one's point of view is right. It only means that this point of view won out in the ancient debate. I am convinced that the future of the Christian faith rests not on reasserting those words of antiquity, but on our ability to refashion the symbols by which Christianity is to be understood in our time. (p. 19)

Brian McLaren, *A New Kind of Christianity*:

> We haven't even begun to resolve all the issues of living in a multifaith world as deeply committed Christians seeking a new kind of Christianity. But I hope this much is clear: there is a way to be a committed follower of Christ that doesn't require you to be flatly and implacably against other religions and their adherents. (p. 223)

Attempting to provide a concrete definition of progressive Christianity is no simple task. Even among its adherents, you will find various opinions, critiques, and lines of demarcation.

Colby Martin, former copastor of the LGBTQ–affirming Sojourn Grace Collective based in Lakeside, California, writes in *The Shift: Surviving and Thriving after Moving from Conservative to Progressive Christianity*: "There does not exist one single way to be a progressive Christian; therefore the following pages won't tell you what you need to do (or worse, what you need to believe) in order to become one."[1]

That said, if progressive Christians cannot agree upon a universal set of principles and commitments that encompass everything they believe and value, I will not attempt to provide you with one. Instead, I defer to the way Roger Wolsey, a United Methodist pastor in Grand Junction, Colorado, defines it in his book *Kissing Fish: Christianity for People Who Don't Like Christianity*:

> Progressive Christianity is an approach to the Christian faith that is influenced by post-liberalism and postmodernism and: proclaims Jesus of Nazareth as Christ, Savior, and Lord; emphasizes the Way and teachings of Jesus, not merely His person; emphasizes God's immanence not merely God's transcendence; leans toward panentheism rather than supernatural theism; emphasizes salvation here and now instead of primarily in heaven later; emphasizes being saved for robust, abundant/eternal life over being saved from hell; emphasizes the social/communal aspects of salvation instead of merely the personal; stresses social justice as integral to Christian discipleship; takes the Bible seriously but not necessarily literally, embracing a more interpretive, metaphorical understanding; emphasizes orthopraxy instead of orthodoxy (right actions over right beliefs); embraces reason as well as paradox and mystery—instead of blind allegiance

to rigid doctrines and dogmas; does not consider homo-sexuality to be sinful; and does not claim that Christianity is the only valid or viable way to connect to God (is non-exclusive).[2]

In the preface of his book *Jesus Was a Liberal*, Unitarian Universalist minister Scotty McLennan remarks that not every liberal or progressive Christian stands for the same thing. However, there are a few "principles" that are most agreed upon.

There are many roads to the top of the spiritual mountain, and Christianity is only one of them. Interfaith understanding and tolerance are critical. We see Jesus primarily as a spiritual and ethical teacher and less as being identical with God. Living a fulfilled and ethical life here and now is more important than speculating on what happens to us after we die.[3]

ProgressiveChristianity.org lists "The Core Values of Progressive Christianity," which reads:

Please take these lightly but seriously. They are not dogma, they are simply a starting point to establish conversations and a foundation of values and beliefs that we have observed Progressive Christians generally share. It's ok if you don't agree with all the words or all the parts. We support your authentic path.

Believe that following the way and teachings of Jesus can lead to experiencing sacredness, wholeness, and unity of all life, even as we recognize that the Spirit moves in beneficial ways in many faith traditions.

Seek community that is inclusive of all people, honoring differences in theological perspective, age, race, sexual orientation, gender identity/expression, class, or ability.

Strive for peace and justice among all people, knowing that behaving with compassion and selfless love towards one another is the fullest expression of what we believe.

Embrace the insights of contemporary science and strive to protect the Earth and ensure its integrity and sustainability.

Commit to a path of life-long learning, believing there is more value in questioning than in absolutes.[4]

One thing that progressive Christians unanimously agree upon is that the Bible is not God's divine authority. According to them, the Bible can be reinterpreted in limitless numbers of ways because of the power of personal experience. People do not just approach the Bible with a blank slate; they come with their own interpretive truth and personal experiences. In other words, they are their own authority.

Progressive Christians make it seem as though it's impossible for anyone to understand who and what Jesus is. They project their altered view of Him as though it is the proper gospel, but at the same time, they like to say that your view of Jesus (whatever it is) is true for you and adds significance to the profile of Him that millions of believers throughout church history have developed.

In a nutshell, most progressive Christians will align with these "beliefs":

- They are reclaiming the "truth" through postmodern thought.[5]
- Mankind did not inherit a sin nature from Adam and Eve.

- The Bible has errors and has been altered many times, and most of it is to be interpreted metaphorically.
- Many paths make up the Oneness of God.
- Social justice is the Gospel.

A New and Improved Christianity?
The Nuances of Progressive Christianity

Placing the term "progressive" in front of "Christian" makes it seem like a "new and improved" version of Christianity. It acts as though it belongs in the same camp as biblical Christianity, but it does not embrace any of its fundamental beliefs.

The truth is, progressive Christians not only sharply oppose biblical Christianity, but do not consider themselves to be biblical Christians. Since progressive Christians predominantly believe the Bible is metaphorical, I could just as easily identify them as "metaphorical Christians."

Let us go a step further: A more accurate label for progressive Christians is "modern religious gnostics." Biblical and progressive Christianity may share a few general commonalities, but that does not mean the two are compatible.

Let me put it bluntly: Progressive Christians are "doctrine deniers." They deny the beliefs, creeds, and doctrinal statements of historic-orthodox Christianity. They make it sound like doctrine gets in the way of our truly knowing Jesus. You will hear them use phrases such as "freeing Jesus from doctrine," "not restricting or limiting Jesus to doctrine," or "doctrine is not the way to know who Jesus truly is."

Diana Butler Bass, a mentor to Jen Hatmaker, writes in *Freeing Jesus*:

I appreciate the theological traditions surrounding the Christ of faith. Yet neither historical scholarship nor conventional doctrine quite captures who Jesus is for me—the skepticism bred by one and the submissiveness inculcated by the other do not fully tell the story of the Jesus I know: the Jesus of experience.[6]

In his classic book *Jesus for the Non-Religious*, Spong openly states that he is "interested in finding Jesus beyond scripture, beyond creeds, and doctrines."[7]

It is impossible to articulate what you believe without establishing a framework of practical doctrines. Doctrines hold Christians accountable to certain beliefs that align with the Word of God and uphold specific behaviors that reflect and honor Jesus Christ. They are not based on rituals or formulas built from philosophical theory; they are formulations of God's historical actions in the world that are experienced by humankind and are articulated by following God's revealed truth.

McGrath correctly observes,

At the heart of the Christian faith stands a person, not a doctrine—but a person who gives rise to doctrine the moment we begin to wrestle with the question, "Who is Jesus Christ?" The idea that we can somehow worship, adore or imitate Jesus Christ without developing doctrines about him is indefensible.[8]

Progressive Christians treat *orthodoxy* (right doctrine) and *orthopraxy* (right living) as though they exist at opposite ends of a spectrum. But you cannot know *how* to live if you do not have moral truths that teach you *what* is right, so in biblical Christianity, the two work hand in hand.

Without familiarizing ourselves with a formulation of doctrines and creeds that illuminate the person of Jesus in the context of Christianity, there is no way to know who He is or how to worship Him correctly. Thus, doctrines are essential truths about Jesus that provide Christians a standard of beliefs that reveal truths about God from Scripture, exalt Him as Lord and Savior, and teach the Church how to pattern their lives in obedience to Him.

I must mention, however, that although the doctrines of Jesus reflect who He is, the limits of human language prevent us from fully appreciating His divine nature.

The fact is, "modern religious gnostics" have more in common with atheists and secularists than they do with biblical Christians.

What does that say about the heart of progressive Christianity?

In the end, progressive Christianity is not "a fresh take on Jesus." It despecializes the Bible, strips Jesus of His divine authority as God, and renders void the Gospel message of original sin and the need for divine atonement.

Keep this in mind as you work through the Christian doctrines relating to Jesus's divinity, virgin birth, miracles, atonement on the cross, resurrection, and Second Coming. As you start unraveling the controversial picture of Jesus progressive Christians paint, I hope you will see how this false religion is uprooting the fabric of historic Christianity and blatantly attempting to overhaul the very identity and integrity of Jesus as it pushes the boundaries of biblical theology

SIX ATTACKS
AGAINST JESUS

Part 2 offers side-by-side comparisons of biblical and progressive Christianity and illustrates the massive doctrinal and theological chasm between their views concerning Jesus's full divinity, virgin birth, miraculous life, substitutionary atonement, bodily resurrection, and Second Coming.

CHAPTER 3

Hijacking Jesus's Divinity

In a very sly way, Robin Meyers writes in *Saving Jesus from the Church* that Jesus taught us to worship God through His example. Meyers appears to be making a valid point.

Progressive Christians build on this foundation by asking questions like, "Aren't we to love others as Jesus loved us?" "Aren't we to follow Jesus's example by not seeking our own selfish desires but by doing the will of God?" "What about when Jesus said in John 5:30, 'I seek not my own will but the will of him who sent me'?" "John 13:15 makes it clear as day that Jesus tells us to follow His example."

That all sounds pretty good—almost convincing. But Meyers and others are actually employing devious tactics that undermine the very divinity of Jesus Christ.

Meyers certainly believes Jesus revealed God to us and believes Him to be the most remarkable person who ever lived[1]—but that's where it stops for him. According to Meyers, Jesus was a man of great faith. Nothing more.

In their book *Living the Questions: The Wisdom of Progressive Christianity*, two leaders of progressive churches, David Felten and Jeff Procter-Murphy, write,

> Christians who want to take Jesus seriously need to take his humanity seriously, for Jesus has revealed what it means to be fully human. By living into the fullness of his humanity, Jesus demonstrated a way of being that could only be described by his early followers as divine. As Athanasius suggested, even in the fourth century, "He became what we are that he might make us what he is."[2]

Felten and Procter-Murphy make it sound as though they are fighting to keep Jesus as the center of Christianity—which, quite frankly, can and does confuse Christians. Progressive Christians can pepper Jesus's humanity with majestic language all they want, but in the end still consider Him only a human being—not the Second Person of the Godhead.

Historical Inquiry of Progressive Christianity

Progressive Jesus scholars' public discussion centers on the Nag Hammadi Manuscripts (AD 250–450)—a collection of twelve Coptic codices containing fifty-two gnostic documents written over 150 years after the New Testament canon closed. They believe one ancient source, the Gospel of Thomas, is an authentic part of the "lost Scriptures" that holds the key to "recapturing" Jesus's glory.

In *Christianity in Blue*, United Church of Christ minister David Kaden writes,

Had I been around when ancient lists of canonical texts were being written, I would have made a forceful case to include the Gospel of Thomas as a fifth gospel in the New Testament.[3]

Tim Freke isn't someone I would refer to as a progressive Jesus scholar, but he is an influencer in progressive scholarship. He has written a book, *Jesus and the Lost Goddess: The Secret Teachings of the Original Christians*, which charts how Christianity got started. Freke's main point is that "the myth of Christianity" came from the goddess Sophia. He believes many of the traditional stories of Jesus are spiritual allegories. In that capacity, Jesus was only a mystic who pointed people to a higher purpose, united in love and harmony.

In *The Jesus Mysteries: Was the "Original Jesus" a Pagan God?*, Freke writes that Christianity sprang from a coverup: The despairing disciples didn't know how to pick up the pieces after their promised savior died a despicable public death. In their plight, several felt they needed to honor their leader by portraying Him not as a defeated warrior, but as a triumphant Savior who remains alive in the hearts of His followers. Therefore, they consolidated images of Jesus in the canonical gospels that mimicked the gods of Greek mythology.

Historical Inquiry of Biblical Christianity

There is early historical evidence that the canonical gospels framed Jesus as God right from the start. Take Mark, for instance, the first gospel written in the mid-50s (known as the "Markan Priority" because it feeds details to the gospels of Matthew and Luke).

In examining the Markan account, literary scholars engineered a technique called "*inclusio*" that builds structure around a section of material or a book of antiquity. (Think of it as marking or high-lighting important themes throughout a particular set of writings.)

The authors of *Reinventing Jesus* elaborate on the use of *inclusio* in Mark's gospel by commenting,

> Consider Mark, which most scholars believe to be the earliest of the four Gospels, written no later than the 60s. Mark opens with the words, "The beginning of the gospel of Jesus Christ, the Son of God" (Mark 1:1) and climaxes with the confession of the Roman centurion attending Jesus' crucifixion: "Truly this man was God's Son!" (Mark 15:39). The inclusio formed by references to Jesus as God's Son suggests that everything between is to be read in light of the belief that Jesus was no mere man. From beginning to end, Mark presents Jesus as the unique Son of God.[4]

The Nag Hammadi documents, on the other hand, are eighth-century writings containing allegedly esoteric teachings of Jesus—but unlike the canonical gospels, they lack specific details that might prove their authenticity.

Many of the leading Church fathers did not regard the gnostic writings as credible sources about Jesus but as mythological writings written to deceive Christians.

In AD 180, Irenaeus, bishop of Lyons, wrote *Against Heresies*, proving the lack of credibility and theological errors in the gnostic documents regarding Jesus. As a former pupil of the Apostle John, he also firmly believed in and defended the divine nature of Christ. He is recorded as stating, "The Father is God and the Son is God; for He who is born of God is God."[5]

Another compelling argument that proves the early Christians affirmed Jesus as God before the Council of Nicea (AD 325) is found in Justin Martyr's *Dialogue with Trypho* (mid-second century).

> Our teacher of these things is Jesus Christ, who also was born for this purpose, and was crucified under Pontius Pilate, procurator of Judaea, in the times of Tiberius Caesar; and that we reasonably worship him, having learned that he is the Son of the true God himself, and holding him in the second place, and the prophetic Spirit in the third, we will prove. For they proclaim our madness to consist in this, that we give to a crucified man a place second to the unchangeable and eternal God, the Creator of all; for they do not discern the mystery that is herein, to which, as we make it plain to you, we pray you to give heed.[6]

Therefore, by the time the Council of Nicea came to order, there was no conspiracy to use it to declare Jesus as God; Christians already affirmed and worshiped Him as such. The purpose of Nicea was to renounce Arianism as unorthodox and to settle on a creed that declared and preserved the full divinity of Jesus Christ. The council unwaveringly acknowledged that Jesus Christ was fully God and fully man using a distinctive elemental phrase: "one Lord Jesus Christ, the only begotten Son of God, Light of Light, Very God of Very God, Begotten, not made."

Several efforts to defend Jesus's full divinity were made throughout early Church history.

- The Athanasian Creed (AD 373) speaks of "neither confounding the Persons *nor dividing the substance*" of the Godhead (Father, Son, and Holy Spirit).

- The Cappadocian Fathers are regarded as notable fourth-century scholars of the doctrine of the Trinity whereby they specified the "Godhead" is not made up of three deities by three distinct personages of the same nature: Father, Son, and Holy Spirit.
- The First Council of Constantinople (AD 381) reaffirmed the Council of Nicea and clearly stated that Jesus was fully divine.
- The Council of Ephesus (AD 431) articulated the full divinity and humanity of Jesus Christ and repudiated Nestorius of Antioch, who taught Jesus was a conjunction of two persons in one body.

Biblical Explanations of Progressive Christianity

Many progressive Jesus scholars, such as John Shelby Spong, Dale Allison, and Diarmaid MacCulloch, don't believe the New Testament presents Jesus as the expected Messiah who fulfilled the prophetic Scriptures. The more compelling and obvious evaluation, they argue, is that the gospel writers made it *seem* as though Jesus fulfilled prophecy.

Spong writes, "A magical view of the gospels was developed which asserted that instead of the Hebrew stories shaping the Jesus story, the events of Jesus' life simply fulfilled biblical expectations and prophecies in some miraculous and preordained way."[7]

Progressive pastors David Felten and Jeff Procter-Murphy dismiss the canonical accounts as "highly subjective, written by individuals speaking to particular communities of believers."[8] In their view, the gospels are not to be respected as historical accounts of Jesus's life—only as records of early Christian traditions.

Progressive Christians think the Bible's Christological accounts are either clouded with uncertainty or were later inserted to elevate Jesus's divine attributes. Former Pittsburgh Theological Seminary professor Dale Allison writes that our "theological tradition is full of tendentious, ahistorical readings of gospel texts, readings that have served orthodox christological agendas instead of historical truth."[9] Therefore, Matthew amended Mark to advance a higher Christology; there was ideological tinkering to John's gospel—and that renders them both unreliable accounts of the life of Jesus.[10]

Consider how Diana Butler Bass interprets the words of Jesus in John 14:6: "I am the way, and the truth, and the life. No one comes to the Father except through me." In her book *Freeing Jesus*, she writes:

> "Way" is not a technique or map, "truth" is not about philosophy or dogma, and "life" is not about going to heaven. In the mystical poetry of John, Jesus uses these terms to explain how he embodies a way of being in this world so close to the heart of God that God can be known in and through Jesus.[11]

For the average progressive Christian, Jesus appears to have acted more as the first Christian who ushered in a new form of religion—and as such, we need to see Him as an example of our faith, not a deity we worship.

Biblical Explanations of Biblical Christianity

Biblical Christianity wholeheartedly affirms that Jesus believed and taught He was God (see John 5:23; 14:6–9; 20:28–29). Perhaps the clearest example is John 10:30–33, in which Jesus's opponents sought to stone Him based on His profession to be "one" with the

Father. Jesus uses the word "one" (ἐν [*hen*]) in the neuter, implying that He and the Father are of the same essence or nature.

Below are three proof texts that convincingly demonstrate that Jesus claimed to be God, which are verified through Scripture's affirmations of Him, as well as His actions and what others said about Him.

Proof Text 1: The Affirmations of Jesus

During His Galilean ministry, Jesus made frequent "I AM" statements that affirmed His claim to be God (see John 17:3–5; 18:4–6).

For example, Jesus used the word *eimi* to emphasize His eternality when He stated to His audience, "Before Abraham was, I AM" (John 8:58). The "I AM" denotes Jesus's active self-existence and eternality. That is equivalent to the word "YHWH" ("I AM") used in Exodus 3:14, when God said to Moses, "I AM WHO I AM." This is highly significant on two accounts. First, Yahweh is a notable name given only to God in the Old Testament. Second, the Bible teaches there is no other God apart from Him (Isaiah 44:6). And finally, God does not share His glory with any others (Isaiah 42:8).

Christ also affirmed He was God in the way He taught. For example, Jesus often prefaced His teachings with the word "Amen" or "Truly" to notify the audience that what He was about to say was true and infallible (Matthew 19:23, 28).

Furthermore, in the Sermon on the Mount, Jesus displayed complete self-authority when He said, "*Ego de Lego*," which means, "But *I* say," pointing to the fact that what He had to say was the final authority and complete revelation of the will of God (Matthew 5:22, 28, 34).

Proof Text 2: The Actions of Christ

The Old Testament contains approximately two hundred predictive prophecies concerning the coming Messiah. Specifically, Psalm 2:7 says, "You are my Son; today I have begotten you." According to this

Messianic passage, God declares Christ to be the begotten Son of God from all eternity. More than seven hundred years before Christ's arrival, Isaiah wrote, "The virgin shall conceive and bear a son, and shall call his name Immanuel" (7:14). Jesus not only fulfilled Isaiah's prophecy of the virgin birth, but *every* significant predictive prophecy recorded in the Old Testament.

- Jesus was born in Bethlehem (Micah 5:2)
- Jesus came from the tribe of Judah (Genesis 49:10)
- Jesus was a direct descendant of King David (2 Samuel 7:16)
- Jesus was born precisely 483 years after the Temple's destruction in 444 BC (Daniel 9:24)

As if fulfilling almost two hundred messianic prophecies wasn't extraordinary enough, Jesus's impeccability is another credible piece of evidence that verifies His divinity. By the time Jesus's trial and crucifixion had concluded, eleven individuals had professed His innocence (Matthew 27:4, 19, 24; Luke 23:15, 41; John 18:38). One of the best-known came from Pilate himself, when he announced before the Jews that he found no fault in Jesus (Matthew 27:24).

Proof Text 3: The Acclaims of Christ

After witnessing Jesus's miracles and contemplating His heavenly teachings, Peter publicly confessed Him to be the "Messiah, the *Son of the Living God*" (Matthew 16:16). The phrase "Son of the Living God" is a referential claim that unites Jesus to the very attributes of God.

In addition to these acclaims, Jesus accepted worship without ever rebuking His followers on at least nine occasions (see Matthew 8:2; 9:18; 14:33; 15:25; 20:20; 28:17; Mark 5:6; John 9:38; 20:28).

Furthermore, Jesus commonly referred to Himself as the "Son of Man" (*ho huios tou anthrōpou*), a direct reference to the prophetic title mentioned by the prophet Daniel (7:13). "Son of Man" appears forty-three times in the New Testament as a distinctive title used chiefly as a signature designation of Christ as God in the flesh.

This not only points to His heavenly origin, it also conveys certain aspects of His earthly ministry and future Kingdom.

Jesus, as the Son of Man, accomplished and fulfilled specific duties and responsibilities that had to come from God alone:

- forgiving people of their sins (John 3; Mark 2:1–12)
- offering them eternal life (John 5:21)
- raising people from the dead (Matthew 9:18–26; Luke 7:11–15; John 11:17–44)
- judging the world (Matthew 25:31–33; John 5:22, 27)
- healing various diseases and sicknesses (Matthew 9:20–22, 27–31; 12:9–13)
- casting out demons (Mark 1:23–28; Matthew 9:32–33)

It is overwhelmingly apparent through the way that Jesus, His disciples, and the way various Bible authors represent Him, that they all believed Him to be God.

Exegetical Examination of Christological Passages in the New Testament

We see the proof texts in the gospels that point to the fact that Jesus is God, but let's explore in more detail some of the New Testament's most widely recognized and unpack their Christological significance.

John 1:1

In the beginning was the Word, and the Word was with God, and the Word was God.

John employs stylistic techniques that are unique to his biography. The heart of everything he writes, from the opening phrase "in the beginning was the Word" to his ending remarks, "there are also many other things that Jesus did" (21:25), all points to the rich tapestry of Jesus's divinity. In his opening, John intentionally alludes to Genesis 1:1 while highlighting the phrase, "and the Word (*Logos*) was with God (*theos*)" to point out the pre-existence of Jesus Christ. John goes from beyond the origin of the universe ("In the beginning") to eternity ("the Word was with God"). He uses the imperfect *ēn* ("was") three times to express God's timeless existence.[12] The word *Logos* was familiar to John's audience, but here, it is a designation given to Jesus Himself. John deliberately structured the first and second clauses to underscore the essence of God. This makes more sense when you read, "the Word became flesh and dwelt among us" (1:14). John uses the same language of God dwelling (tabernacling) with Israel in the wilderness as Jesus coming into the world. Thus, according to the Apostle John, Jesus—God the Son—is fully God.

John 20:28–29

Thomas answered him, "My Lord and my God!" Jesus said to him, "Have you believed because you have seen me? Blessed are those who have not seen and yet have believed."

What makes Thomas's confession so extraordinary is that he was skeptical about Jesus being resurrected at first—but when he saw the risen Jesus, he believed. A. T. Robertson, a renowned Greek scholar and author of *Word Pictures in the New Testament*, confirms that the phrase "My Lord and my God (ὁ κυριος μου και ὁ θεος μου [*Ho kurios mou kai ho theos mou*]) it is not merely an exclamation, but Thomas personally addressing 'the Risen Christ as Lord and God.'"[13]

Each section of John's gospel attests to Jesus's divinity: (1) preincarnate state (1:1), (2) incarnate state (1:18), and (3) postresurrection state (20:28).[14] John ends by stating,

> Now Jesus did many other signs in the presence of the disciples, which are not written in this book; but these are written so that you may believe that Jesus is the Christ, the Son of God, and that by believing you may have life in his name. (20:30–31)

Philippians 2:6–11

> Who, though he was in the form of God, did not count equality with God a thing to be grasped, but emptied himself, by taking the form of a servant, being born in the likeness of men. And being found in human form, he humbled himself by becoming obedient to the point of death, even death on a cross. Therefore God has highly exalted him and bestowed on him the name that is above every name, so that at the name of Jesus every knee should bow, in heaven and on earth and under the earth, and every tongue confess that Jesus Christ is Lord, to the glory of God the Father.

Paul says that Jesus "humbled himself." The word he uses is *kenosis*. What Paul means is that Jesus temporarily surrendered the independent exercise of or voluntarily limited certain divine attributes while occupying human form. In his book *Jesus Christ Our Lord*, John F. Walvoord explains it by saying:

> The act of kenosis . . . may be properly understood to mean that Christ surrendered no attribute of Deity, but that He did voluntarily restrict their independent use in keeping with His purpose of living among men and their limitations.[15]

A proper exegetical study of this passage is necessary to provide an accurate interpretation of the kenosis theory. First, in Philippians 2:6, Paul distinctively affirms Jesus's full divinity by writing, "[Jesus] *being* in the very *form* of God, did not consider it equality with God." Paul's use of the word "being" (ὑπαρχων [*huparchōn*]) is in the present active participle, implying that Jesus not only *is* the eternal God (prior to the Incarnation) but also *continues to be* God during and after the Incarnation.

Moreover, the word "form" or "nature" (ἐν μορφῃ θεου [*en morphēi theou*]) in verse six means "intrinsic" or "essential" form or attributes of God. Walvoord delivers this analysis of the word *morphēi*:

> As it related to the eternal deity of Christ, it refers to the fact that Christ in eternity past in outer appearance manifested His divine attributes. It was not mere form or appearance, but that which corresponded to what He was eternally.[16]

Jesus has always possessed the essential divinity of God from all eternity, even while holding the status of human for over three decades on Earth.

Paul also uses various unambiguous idioms, such as: "form of a bondservant," "likeness of man," "appearance of man," and "point of death" to convey the addition of humanity without the subtraction of deity. The great theologian Millard Erickson maintains that

> It appears that there are both a positive parallelism with "equality with God," thus making "the form of God" a strong statement of deity, and an adversative parallelism with "the form of a servant," thus forming a contrast.[17]

Theological Arguments of Progressive Christianity

The late theologian John B. Cobb Jr. taught that God is "in process" with the world. In other words, as God changes, so do we. We are becoming one with God as He becomes one with us.[18]

Progressive Christians have built on the teachings of process theology and describe God in panentheistic terms, i.e., God is in all things and all things are in God. In 2011, Disciples of Christ minister Robert Cornwall posted a long excerpt from Bruce G. Epperly's book, *Why Progressive Christianity Needs Process Theology*, that included the statement, "God embraces all things experientially, but is more than all things, in God's ongoing experience and shaping of reality."[19]

Therefore, the person of Jesus was enraptured in the Oneness of God but was not God.

Richard Rohr, considered one of the godfathers of progressive Christianity, wrote one of the best books explaining process theology and panentheism, *The Universal Christ*. Rohr writes,

What if Christ is a name for the transcendent within of every "thing" in the universe? What if Christ is a name for the immense spaciousness of all true Love? What if Christ refers to an infinite horizon that pulls us from within and pulls us forward too? What if Christ is another name for everything—in its fullness?[20]

By the fourth and fifth centuries, progressive Christians say, the church had "systematized" Jesus's divinity, giving credence to the "detrimental" doctrine that complete salvation is found only in and through Him.[21]

They claim the Councils of Nicea installed medieval bishops in order to reduce the influence of early Christianity and produce a whole new level of "orthodoxy" for future generations. More to the point, the Councils were more political than theological—giving rise to what Robert Funk, in his book *Honest to Jesus*, calls "creedal Christianity."[22]

The gist of progressive Christian theology is to see Jesus as a devout Jew who revolutionized the religion and teachings of His day. The moment we erect Jesus as God to be revered and worshiped, they say we strip Him of His humanity and lessen His life's impact on us as we do the moral good He would want us to do in this life.

Maurice Casey *From Jewish Prophet to Gentile God*	Jesus went from a Jewish leader to being christened a god
John Hick *The Myth of God Incarnate*	Jesus as God is metaphorical
E. P. Sanders *Jesus and Judaism*	Jesus, a follower of John the Baptist, created an eschatological movement
John P. Meier *A Marginal Jew*	Jesus was an eschatological prophet
Dale Allison *The Historical Christ and the Theological Jesus*	Jesus was a profound Jewish teacher whose parables enriched people's lives
Richard Rohr *The Universal Christ*	Jesus, or the Cosmic Christ, embodied the spirit that is in everything

Theological Arguments of Biblical Christianity

Despite what progressive Christians say, Jesus's divinity is front and center in the New Testament.

Jesus Existed before Coming into the World

Several complementary passages in the Bible illustrate the pre-incarnate Christ:

- Jesus openly tells Nicodemus that He "came down from heaven" (John 3:13).
- Jesus prays to the Father, "Glorify Me in Your own presence with the glory that I had with You *before the world existed*" (John 17:5, italics mine), and declares to the disciples that He "came down from heaven" (John 6:38).
- John the Baptist testifies to Christ's eternality when he cries out, "He who comes after me has surpassed me because *he was before me*" (John 1:15, 30, italics mine).
- Micah states that Christ is "from old to everlasting" (Micah 5:2), while the prophet Isaiah said the Messiah would be the "Everlasting Father" (Isaiah 9:6).

Walvoord summarizes the significance of these references to the pre-incarnate Jesus:

> His preincarnate works of creation, providence, preservation and His promises in eternity past, the appearances of Christ in the Old Testament, and the many other intimations of preexistence combine to form a massive proof that Christ existed before His birth in Bethlehem.[23]

Jesus's Two Natures

The term used to describe Jesus's two natures is "hypostatic union." The phrase, *kath hypostasin enosis* (hypostatic union), comes from Cyril's *Second Letter to Nestorius*, in which he wrote, "the Logos united flesh to Himself." It also appears in *Five Tomes against the Blasphemies of Nestorius*, as well as in the Westminster Confession (VIII.II):

> Two whole, perfect, and distinct natures, the Godhead and the manhood, were inseparably joined together in one person, without conversion, composition, or confusion.[24]

To better understand this, it's important to distinguish between *person* and *nature*.

Jesus isn't a compound person with a split personality. He was one person operating uniquely in two natures: one divine and one human. These are indissolubly united without mixture and without losing their unique characteristics.[25] That is, there was no corruption or diminution of divinity or humanity in Him. Each nature perfectly retains its distinctive qualities and maintains its unique integrity in the person of Jesus Christ.

If either had crossed into the other, then humanity would become eternal, and divinity would become noneternal. This would contradict the laws of nature—God as Creator and man as the created. One cannot become the other.

Spiritual Results of Progressive Christianity

After everything is said and done, what is left of Jesus in progressive Christianity? What kind of spiritual life do progressive Christians have if they don't worship Jesus as God?

In *Freeing Jesus*, Diana Butler Bass refers to Jesus as "the fair, lovely word 'Mother,'"[26] and depicts Him as "the shekhinah." "Precious and lovely are the children of grace in the sight of our heavenly Mother."[27]

In 2012, Peter Enns wrote a blog post titled "Jesus Had a Fallen Nature, Just Like the Bible" in which he writes,

Let me summarize this in my own way. The question, it seems to me, is how comfortable are we with the incarnation and its implications? How truly human a Jesus do we want? Can our theology really handle a Jesus and a Bible that so thoroughly reflect back to us the cultural perspectives of the time? Or, would we rather have a Jesus and a Bible that keeps [*sic*] their distance from the human condition?"[28]

Jesus, in the end, is an example to help build out our own spiritual path with God as we attempt to live a life of peace and do the common good, as He did before His tragic death.

Spiritual Results of Biblical Christianity

Jesus is the central figure of Christianity, of life, and of all eternity.

As Josh and Sean McDowell write in their book, *Evidence That Demands a Verdict*,

If Jesus is Lord, people are obligated to follow him or else honestly reject him and be held responsible accordingly. Therein lies the greatest challenge.[29]

The Apostle Paul put it beautifully when he penned these words to a beloved friend:

For the grace of God has appeared, bringing salvation for all people, training us to renounce ungodliness and worldly passions, and to live self-controlled, upright, and godly lives in the present age, waiting for our blessed hope, the appearing of the glory of our great God and Savior

Jesus Christ, who gave himself for us to redeem us from all lawlessness and to purify for himself a people for his own possession who are zealous for good works. (Titus 2:11–14)

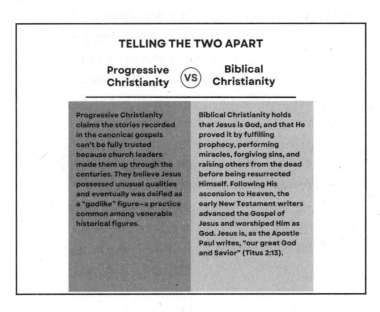

TELLING THE TWO APART

Progressive Christianity (VS) **Biblical Christianity**

Progressive Christianity	Biblical Christianity
Progressive Christianity claims the stories recorded in the canonical gospels can't be fully trusted because church leaders made them up through the centuries. They believe Jesus possessed unusual qualities and eventually was deified as a "godlike" figure—a practice common among venerable historical figures.	Biblical Christianity holds that Jesus is God, and that He proved it by fulfilling prophecy, performing miracles, forgiving sins, and raising others from the dead before being resurrected Himself. Following His ascension to Heaven, the early New Testament writers advanced the Gospel of Jesus and worshiped Him as God. Jesus is, as the Apostle Paul writes, "our great God and Savior" (Titus 2:13).

Key Points to Use When Talking to Progressive Christians

Jesus is more than a god-like character with special powers. He is the Second Person of the Godhead. He is God! So, keep these main points at the center of your convos when talking to a progressive Christian about Jesus's divinity:

- **Historical:** The Gnostic writings are not reliable records of Jesus. They were written far later and do not align with the structure and beliefs of the canonical gospels.
- **Biblical:** The canonical gospels are early, accurate accounts that do not carry any exaggerations, but record

Jesus's personal claims to be God, testify to His sinless life and miraculous fulfillment of prophecy, and authenticate His divine status.

- **Theological:** Jesus isn't "in process with the rest of the world." He resides over the universe and has absolute power and authority over it. The New Testament writers reveal that though He was human, His physical appearance revealed the very presence of God on Earth.

- **Spiritual:** Jesus didn't become a "finite god." In the incarnation, He took on a second nature, making a way to restore His creation to Himself. Therefore, we unequivocally worship Him and confess, affirm, teach, and proclaim that Jesus Christ is Lord and Savior!

CHAPTER 4

Hijacking Jesus's

Virgin Birth

"**I** no longer believe in the virgin birth," said Chris, rather dismissively.

I was surprised. Chris had always been a diligent Christian who studied the Bible and kept himself grounded in theology.

"Chris, what would you say is the main reason you now reject it?" I asked.

"It's nothing more than a contrived tale later invented by Christians as an overclaim of Jesus's deity," he replied, a touch bitterly. "It makes absolutely no sense to say Jesus became human if He's God." I could feel the tension oozing from him.

I knew whatever I said next would determine how that conversation went. We discussed some of the YouTube videos from progressive Christians that influenced his thinking. Fortunately, he was open to discussing the theological significance of Jesus's virgin birth, and at the end of our conversation admitted he still needed to examine the evidence.

I will tell you what I shared with him: If the virgin birth is dubious, as most progressive Christians believe, then the entire Christian faith is untrue.

That's why you need to understand the way progressives deny the virgin birth and become competent in your ability to defend its theological importance.

The first thing to understand is that progressive Christians think the story of the virgin birth is detrimental to the faith. In his last public address, the late Bishop John Shelby Spong told a packed audience at the Chautauqua Institution in 2011, "Doctrines such as the incarnation and the Trinity can never again pretend to define God or Jesus. Can the Church set these things aside without cutting all ties to what is traditionally called historic Christianity? I think we can. And I think we must."[1]

Some progressive Christians would even say their faith is *more* reverent because their modern reasoning and intellect prevent them from believing in fanciful stories that contradict science.

Either the Virginal Conception is a bogus claim the disciples made up to make Jesus seem more remarkable than He was, or it's true. Here's how the two sides of the debate shape up.

Historical Inquiry of Progressive Christianity

Progressive Christians claim that the virgin birth story was an invention added to Jesus's story after the fact, eventually becoming a weighty doctrine that set the stage for His divinity.

Here are three historical inquiries progressive Christians cite in efforts to disprove the Virginal Conception.

The Gnostic Writings

The Gospel of Thomas (AD 140–180), the Gospel of Judas (second century), and the Gospel of Philip (fourth century) are the main ones used to deny the virgin birth. Religious historian Elaine Pagels claims the Gospel of Thomas is one of the most accurate accounts of Jesus because it was written before the canonical gospels.[2] Many progressive Christians maintain that to know who Jesus is truly, you need to see Him through the lens of this book.

Jesus's Divine Birth Is Invented

Bishop John Shelby Spong contends in *Jesus for the Non-Religious*,

> Both the Bethlehem birthplace and the virgin birth tradition are aspects of a developing interpretive process that did not begin to manifest itself inside the Christian written tradition until well into the ninth decade, or some fifty to sixty years after the earthly life of Jesus had come to an end.[3]

Therefore, progressives say, the virgin story is neither original to Jesus nor factually or biblically true. Christianity, they say, is an amalgamation of other religions that prospered prior to Jesus coming on the scene in Nazareth.

The Virgin Story Is an Ancient Cover-Up

In *Jesus: A New Vision*, Whitley Strieber sets forth what he believes is the most convincing line of reasoning to refute the biblical story of Jesus's virgin birth. At the risk of oversimplifying his argument, I have listed his main points on the following page.

1. The canonical gospels lack firsthand knowledge and therefore are unreliable accounts of Jesus.	2. Early gospels developed Jesus as the Messiah.
3. Jesus's birth mimics that of Moses.	4. Jesus was possibly born out of wedlock.
5. Pantera, a Roman soldier, could more likely be Jesus's father.	6. Celsus tells of an angel impregnating Mary to cover up her affair with Pantera.
8. Mark reveals Jesus as an illegitimate child, so Matthew tries to correct that impression by painting Jesus as Messiah.	9. Jesus's virgin birth story is a copycat of Adonis, Mithras, and Emperor Augustus (supposedly conceived by a giant serpent that impregnated his mother, Atia).[4]
10. Matthew improperly translates "virgin" in Isaiah 7:14 to make it seem as though Mary was, in fact, a virgin.	11. Matthew hides the fact that the magi were a cult that worshiped the Persian god Mithra.

Strieber writes,

So either he was born of a disgraced woman whose husband was an illiterate carpenter but nonetheless somehow acquired incredible learning, or he was of higher birth and the story of the humble carpenter was put about during his lifetime to protect him and his family, and picked up as true by the gospel authors, who knew only the public narrative and were unaware of the secret it concealed.[5]

Giles Fraser, a priest in London and contributor to the British newspaper *The Guardian*, wrote in an article that "the story of the virgin birth runs against the grain of Christianity," claiming that Mary either had consensual sex with Pantera or was raped. In either case, his overarching point is that the later installment of Mary's virginity was an effort to suppress sex and femininity in the early Church.[6]

Another shocking attempt to refute Mary's divine pregnancy by the power of the Holy Spirit comes from Dr. Leslie Weatherhead, who served as pastor at London's City Temple. In his book *The Agnostic Christian*, Weatherhead contends that Mary consented to a "sacred marriage"—a pagan practice that involved a high priest having sex with a virgin to symbolize the union between the sun god and earth goddess—after receiving a vision from an angel about her pregnancy. "Sacred marriages" would produce a child that would be considered "divine." Weatherhead goes so far as to claim Zechariah—Mary's cousin Elizabeth's husband and the father of John the Baptist—was the high priest in question.[7]

Historical Inquiry of Biblical Christianity

The arguments progressive Christians use are nothing new. For centuries, the Church has come under fire from heretics and counterfactual movements that have sought to undermine its validity and vitality in the culture.

As you shall see in this section, there are reasonable answers that prove the virgin birth to be an original story in the life of Jesus and accurately recorded in the canonical gospels.

The first piece of evidence is that the records of the virgin birth were written early.

Mark	Written in the early to mid-50s
Matthew	Written in the mid-50s
Luke	Written in the late 50s/early 60s
John	Written in the late 60s

In the second century, Melito, the bishop of Sardis (near Smyrna), wrote *Pascha*, an early defense of Jesus as the Messiah who fulfilled Old Testament prophecy. Melito also wrote *Discourse on the Cross*, an elaborative affirmation of Jesus's divinity and humanity.[8] In *Discourse on Body and Soul*, he writes,

> For this reason did the Father send His Son from heaven without a bodily form, that, when He should put on a body by means of the Virgin's womb, and be born man, He might save man, and gather together those members of His which death had scattered when he divided man.[9]

The renowned church historian Eusebius of Caesarea references many of Melito's works in his fourth-century work, *Church History*.

More recently, my friend and former cold-case homicide detective J. Warner Wallace compiled a list of things a few of the top Church fathers said about Jesus's virgin birth:[10]

- **Ignatius (AD 35–117, the third Bishop and Patriarch of Antioch)** "He was truly born of a virgin" ("Letter to the Smyrnaeans," ch. 1, written ca. AD 103)
- **Justin Martyr (AD 100–165, early Christian apologist)** "But you (Jews) and your teachers venture to claim that in the prophecy of Isaiah it is not said, 'Behold the virgin will conceive,' but, 'Behold, the young woman will conceive, and bear a son.' Furthermore, you explain the prophecy as if (it referred) to Hezekiah, who was your king. Therefore, I will endeavor to soon discuss this point in opposition to you." (*Dialogue with Trypho*, ch. XLIII, written ca. AD 160)
- **Irenaeus (AD 115–202, the Bishop of Lugdunum)** "Christ Jesus, the Son of God, because of His surpassing love towards his creation, humbled himself to be born of the virgin. Thereby, He united man through Himself to God." (*Against Heresies*, IV.II, written ca. AD 180)
- **Clement of Alexandria (AD 150–215, Christian theologian)** " . . . Jesus, whom of the lightning flash of Divinity the virgin bore." (*Paedagogus*, book I, written ca. AD 195)
- **Tertullian (AD 160–220, Christian apologist)** "This ray of God, then, as it was always foretold in ancient time, descended into a certain virgin, And He was made flesh in her womb. So, in His birth, God and man were united." (*Apology*, ch. XXI, written ca. AD 195)
- **Origen (AD 185–254, Christian apologist and theologian)** "A sign has been given to the house of David. For the virgin conceived, was pregnant, and brought forth a son." (*Contra Celsus*, book I, written ca. AD 225)

In *Contra Celsus*, Origen offered an apologetic rebuttal to Celsus—a pagan philosopher who engineered the scandalous story that Jesus was an illegitimate child[11]—demonstrating that Matthew's storyline of Jesus's birth and early life was written far earlier and is a more established account that provides specific details, unlike Celsus's *The True Word*, which he wrote late in the second century.

When you put Celsus's alleged facts alongside Matthew's corroborated reports, it is apparent that Celsus was trying to discredit Jesus's birth through fabrication.[12]

Matthew	Celsus
Jesus is included in the line of David	Jesus's mother is a poor country woman
Mary's pregnancy is not exposed	Mary is convicted of adultery
Mary is not divorced	Mary is driven out
The child is the Son of God	Father is Pantera
Jesus's birth is heralded by angels	Jesus is born secretly
The family flees to Egypt	Jesus hires himself out in Egypt
Jesus performs miracles	Jesus learns magical powers

Progressive Christians completely overlook Judaism's beliefs, traditions, and social structures. There is no way a God-fearing Jew would buy into the idea of Jesus as Messiah if His virgin birth story had been linked to Greek mythology (syncretism).

The fact remains it is too hard to fabricate events so close to the physical location where they took place: the heart of Jerusalem.

The second piece of evidence is the Gnostic writings are inaccurate sources. Progressive Christians love to cite the Gospel of Thomas to undermine the canonical gospels—but it and the other Gnostic writings in the Nag Hammadi collection are noncanonical books for a good reason. First, the Gospel of Thomas was written long after Jesus's death and is not historically verifiable. Second, the esoteric language throughout its 114 sayings dismisses the atonement of Christ. Third, it states that Jesus teaches His disciples to find the kingdom of God within themselves. This clearly undermines the canonical gospels' teachings on the Kingdom of Heaven. Fourth, its structure is cryptic and contradicts the early narratives of the synoptic gospels. Fifth, in the Gnostic writings, Jesus does not perform any miracles, and never once claims to be God or fulfill prophetic Scripture. Sixth, early Church fathers (Hippolytus, Origen, Eusebius, and Cyril) rejected the Gospel of Thomas as heresy.

The third piece of evidence is that the virgin birth is a credible story, not repackaged paganism. The way progressive Christians depict Jesus's birth almost sounds like a sci-fi film, basically claiming that Christianity is a "copycat" religion that steals from Greek mythology.

J. Ed Komoszewski, founder and director of Christus Nexus, responds to these flagrant attacks by saying:

The Christian message did not plagiarize the writings of pagan religions. There is no substantiated connection between belief in the virgin birth and resurrection of Christ with the cults of Osiris, Dionysus, or Mithra. Alleged parallels between earlier religions and Christianity are not sustainable when the evidence is fairly examined.[13]

The following charts lay out the details of the myths progressive Christians say early Church fathers copied.

ADONIS	DIONYSUS	ATTIS
CLAIM: He was born of a virgin mother (Myrrha). He was crucified and rose from the dead.	**CLAIM:** Born of a virgin.	**CLAIM:** A savior who was slain. The Divine Son of the Father.
FACTS OF THE TALE: A Greek symbol of harvest seasons. One source mentions Adonis dying by Ares, who is disguised as a boar. Parallel references comparing Adonis to Jesus don't come until late in the second century.	**FACTS OF THE TALE:** Conceived by a mortal, Semele, and the Greek god Zeus.	**FACTS OF THE TALE:** Sources describe Attis going insane, castrating himself, and bleeding out in the wilderness. His resurrection story doesn't appear until AD 150.

MITHRAS	HORUS	OSIRIS
CLAIM: A mythological Persian deity that was buried for three days and rose again.	**CLAIM:** The "Sun God of Egypt" was born on Dec. 25 from a virgin and later crucified.	**CLAIM:** Buried for three days.
FACTS OF THE TALE: He was born from a rock. Only secondhand sources with three versions and little proof to back anything up.	**FACTS OF THE TALE:** Horus was born from Isis and Osiris. A mythological figure based on cycles of nature, not on historical facts. (Note: Dec. 25 is not an actual date for Jesus's birth.)	**FACTS OF THE TALE:** Some accounts say Osiris was laid in the Nile and brought back to life by Isis, eventually becoming a god of the underworld. No mention of a three-day burial and resurrection.

Furthermore, neither Matthew nor Luke portray Jesus as a hybrid—half-god and half-man—demigod.

A closer look at the Matthean (1:18–25) and Lukan (1:26–38) birth narratives reveals their differences from Greek and Babylonian mythology. Both Matthew and Luke chart history, bear historical facts surrounding the places and culture in which Jesus's teachings and healings took place, and identify eyewitnesses who also saw them (see Luke 1:1–4). Pagan literature does not.

Oxford University historian Robin Lane Fox asserts that nearly all the supposed parallels between pagan practices and Christianity are spurious. He challenges the thesis that Christianity was "not so very novel in the pagan world." His research led him to conclude that there is, in Leon McKenzie's words, only "a marginal and weak connection between paganism and Christianity."[14]

The bottom line is that no archaeological evidence supports the idea that pagan/Hellenistic religions heavily influenced the Jews in first-century Palestine. Nor do we see anything in the Pauline epistles (as well as his counterparts) of Greek philosophy as the source of their thoughts or beliefs.

Biblical Explanations of Progressive Christianity

How do progressive Christians interpret the virgin birth narrative in the Bible? Here are four common ways.

The Virgin Birth Story Is Metaphorical

In his classic piece, *Jesus: Uncovering the Life, Teachings, and Relevance of a Religious Revolutionary*, Marcus J. Borg says the vast majority of mainstream biblical scholars see these stories as metaphorical narratives rather than as history remembered."[15]

The Word Used for "Virgin" Is a Mistranslation

Robin Meyers writes, "Matthew seeks to ground his story in the Hebrew Scriptures and offers a Greek translation of Isaiah 7:14, which had nothing whatsoever to do with biological virginity."[16] Meyers and other progressives argue that the original Hebrew text used *almah* ("a young girl of marriageable status")—not *bethulah*, which can mean "young girl" or "virgin." Therefore, the exclusive use of the Greek word "virgin" (*parthenos*) in Matthew 1:23 is an incorrect translation.[17]

Joseph Is a Fictitious Character

Meyers writes,

> It is believed by many scholars that Joseph, if he is not a fic-
> tional character altogether, died before the public ministry of
> Jesus began, in part because he is not mentioned at all during
> that ministry, even though Jesus' mother and siblings are. . . .
> The idea that he was an old man when he married Mary is
> pure invention, created perhaps to add plausibility to a later
> tradition about her perpetual virginity.[18]

Paul Does Not Mention the Virgin Birth

Progressive pastors David Felten and Jeff Procter-Murphy advance
the belief that Romans 1 and Galatians 4 do not mention Jesus's
divine virgin birth. They argue that both Mark and Paul most likely
had no factual information that pointed to Jesus's birth as miraculous.[19] Given that the virgin birth carried such divine implications,
Paul would have expounded on such details if they were true. But
considering the virgin birth is absent from the Pauline epistles, it
makes a strong case that Jesus had a normal birth with no angels
appearing from heaven.

Biblical Explanations of Biblical Christianity

The virgin birth story is historically accurate.

Despite the facts progressive Christians deny surrounding Jesus's
birth, most modern scholars believe (as the canonical gospels affirm)
that He was born in Bethlehem (Matthew 2:1).

New Testament scholar Mark Strauss emphasizes Luke's skilled
approach to writing his gospel account.

Luke shows a strong interest in . . . history writing, claiming to be drawing from eyewitness accounts and to have carefully investigated these events himself (1:1–4). [He] dates the gospel with reference to Roman history, identifying key rulers and religious leaders (cf. 1:5; 2:1–3; 3:1–2) . . . [Luke's] interest . . . is in showing the historical veracity and worldwide significance of these events.[20]

Furthermore, although Matthew's and Luke's gospel narratives are historically accurate, neither intended to chronicle Jesus's birth story as a comprehensive commentary. Instead, the birth narratives are measured introductions of the theological significance of Jesus as the Son of God.[21]

Despite what progressives claim, the gospels correctly translate the word "virgin." More than seven hundred years before Christ's arrival, Isaiah prophesied, "The virgin shall conceive and bear a son, and shall call his name Immanuel" (7:14). The word "virgin" in Hebrew is *almah,* and the only meaning it carries in the Old Testament is a marriageable girl who has not had sexual intercourse (see Genesis 24:43; Psalm 68:25; Song of Solomon 6:8). The other Hebrew word is *bethulah,* but Isaiah doesn't use it because *bethulah* doesn't always mean "unmarried woman" or virgin (Esther 2:17; Ezekiel 23:3; Joel 1:8).

In this context, a "virgin" will unnaturally conceive a child, which explains why Isaiah used *almah.* Luke, therefore, links Mary to that young unmarried virgin who would be charged to give birth to the Son of God (see 1:27). In 1:34, after receiving the news from the angel Gabriel, Mary responds with trepidation, and asks, "How will this be, since I am a *virgin?*" [emphasis added]. The Greek word for "virgin" is *parthenos* (which comes from the LXX, the earliest Greek translation of the Hebrew Scriptures) and means "no sexual relations." The writers were particular to Isaiah 7:14 because they knew this was a prophetic reference to the Messiah (see Matthew 1:23). Upon examining the literary context of the Hebrew words *almah* and *bethulah* and the Greek word *parthenos*, the *Lexham Bible Dictionary* has confirmed that "both the Hebrew and Greek terms can refer to either sexual status, age, or both, and are therefore alternatively translated as 'virgin' or 'young woman.'"[22]

In his exegetical work *The Life of Christ*, M. S. Mills examines the use of the word "virgin" in the gospels to extract its purest meaning, concluding that there are "eleven clear gospel assertions of the virgin birth in Jesus' prenatal record."[23]

Mills proceeds to list the various accounts:

> Mary is specifically referred to as a virgin in Luke 1:27 and Matt 1:23; her virginity is defined in Luke 1:34 and Matt 1:25; it is alluded to in Luke 1:49 and Matt 1:16; the Holy Spirit's sole responsibility for Jesus' conception is clearly asserted in Luke 1:31, 35 and Matt 1:20; and the miraculous nature of Jesus' conception is emphasized in Luke 1:37. . . . The Greek texts of Matthew and Luke both use "Parthenos" (virgin) in describing Mary, and not "korasion" or "paidiskee" (maid or damsel), words which Matthew and Luke use elsewhere. So, on word choice alone, the New Testament appears more specific than the Old; but, in any event, these two Gospels also make it plain that Mary "had not known a man" (Luke 1:34) and Joseph "did not know her" until after Jesus was born (Matt 1:25).[24]

The only confusion over Mary's virginity, Mills says, is caused by someone rejecting the verbal inspiration of Scripture.

Resolving the Apparent Contradictions
in the Genealogies of Jesus

Progressive Christians like to say there are contradictions in the two genealogies of Jesus. Matthew's and Luke's genealogies are different, but that does not mean they contradict each other; they are aimed at different audiences, and therefore, start at different points of history. Matthew's audience is the Jews—making it paramount to highlight Jesus as the Messiah. That explains why his genealogy starts with Abraham (Genesis 12 and 15) and goes to David (2 Samuel 7). Luke is writing to give an "orderly account" that focuses on Jesus as the Son of Man—so it makes sense that his genealogy begins with Adam and goes to David.

When the genealogies arrive at David, they split with David's sons. Matthew traces Jesus's line through David's son Solomon (1:6), while Luke traces it through David's son Nathan (3:31). In fact, between David and Jesus, the only names the genealogies have in common are Shealtiel and Zerubbabel (Matthew 1:12; Luke 3:27); most scholars believe these people had the same names but were different individuals. When David's kingdom was separated following Solomon's reign, the Kingdom of Judah (with its capital in Jerusalem) and the kingdom of Israel (capital in Samaria) had specific requirements. Israel stated the king had to be of prophetic or divine appointment (see 1 Kings), while Judah stated the king had to be of Davidic descent (Isaiah 8:9–15; 2 Samuel 7). Therefore, two genealogies were necessary.

Matthew's Genealogy: The Royal Line (Joseph's Side)
Jewish Audience

- Demonstrate Jesus's rightful place on the throne of David

- Calls Jesus the "Son of David" (King) and the "Son of Abraham" (Jew) (1:1)
- Details Jesus's lineage through His legal father, Joseph (Matthew 1:16), not His biological father. There are forty-one generations in all (divided into three sections)
- Focuses on specific accounts and visions of Joseph

Luke's Genealogy: The Levirate Line (Mary's Side) Gentile Audience

- Stems from Mary's line; notice how the opening accounts revolve around her
- Calls Jesus the "Son of Adam" (Man) and the "Son of God" (God) (3:38)
- Provides seventy-seven generations in total. Listing a woman's family tree was against tradition (according to the Talmud).
- Omits names and mentions no women, sticking strictly to Jewish procedures. But to identify that this genealogy is Mary's, the definite article "the" is missing from Joseph's name (all the other names have a definite article). This is an important distinction in Greek because it indicates this is not the line of Joseph, but Mary.

John and Paul's Silence on the Virgin Birth

Let us broaden our knowledge of the "absence" of the virgin birth in John's gospel and Paul's epistles to respond adequately to progressive Christianity.

First, John's gospel mentions Jesus existing in eternity past (1:1) and that Jesus took on a second nature: humanity (1:14). Throughout his gospel, he describes Jesus "coming from heaven" (3:31; 6:38; 8:23), while in other references, he mentions Jesus's human birth (19:37) and that his mother was Mary (2:1; 19:25). John's testimony bears witness to the fact that Jesus's conception came through supernatural intervention.

Second, Paul probably did not bring up the virgin birth as much if it was common knowledge.

Third, Paul's traveling companion, Luke, wrote a detailed account of Jesus's birth (Luke 2). If Paul believed Luke was in error, he would have addressed it in one of his letters.

Fourth, in Galatians 4:4, Paul writes, "But when the fullness of time had come, God sent forth his Son, born of woman, born under the law." Notice that Paul does not mention Joseph, only Mary—a strong indication that he knew Joseph was not Jesus's father because virgin conception was by and through the power of the Holy Spirit. This can be observed in Luke 2:7, where Luke only mentions Mary giving birth to "her firstborn son." Thus, it would seem Paul is uniformly tracking with Luke.

In Romans 1:3, Paul writes, "concerning his Son, who was descended from David according to the flesh." The progressive Christian insists that the "descendent" Paul refers to is Joseph. However, as we saw in the Lukan genealogy, Mary also descended from King David. Furthermore, the term "seed" Paul uses does not infer a biological or paternal lineage.[25]

Lastly, though Paul implied but did not explicitly mention the "virgin birth," he affirms the pre-existence of Jesus in Philippians 2:5–7. It becomes clear that if Paul believed Jesus existed before coming into the world and "taking the form of a servant," it is safe to conclude that Galatians 4:4 and Romans 1:3 refer to Jesus's fulfillment of messianic prophecy (which implies the virgin birth).

Theological Arguments of Progressive Christianity

James Tabor taught Christian origins and ancient Judaism at the University of North Carolina–Charlotte for over thirty years. He would not classify himself as a "progressive Christian" or claim any specific religion (per se). He is, however, a prominent figurehead within progressive Christianity.

In his most recognizable book, *The Jesus Dynasty: The Hidden History of Jesus, His Royal Family, and the Birth of Christianity*, Tabor refers to the virgin birth as Christianity's "fundamental theological dogma"—which is problematic for him.

> But history, by its very nature, is an open process of inquiry that cannot be bound by dogmas of faith. Historians are obliged to examine whatever evidence we have, even if such discoveries might be considered shocking or sacrilegious to some. The assumption of the historian is that all human beings have both a biological mother and father, and that Jesus is no exception. That leaves two possibilities—either Joseph or some other unnamed man was the father of Jesus.[26]

Like most progressive Christians, Tabor rules out the virgin birth story because there is no actual historiographical explanation to back up its claims.

"Birth stories are always fanciful," says Spong. "They are never historical. No one waits outside a maternity ward for a great person to be born."[27]

Moreover, say Felten and Procter-Murphy, the virgin birth was a manipulative theology that parodied a coercive version of God on High that produced more restrictive doctrines that hinder people from knowing Him.[28]

Theological Arguments of Biblical Christianity

The term *incarnation* stems from Latin origin and means to "become in the flesh." Though it is not in the Bible, its scriptural truth and reality are presented in the history and fulfillment of Jesus Christ.

The doctrine of incarnation has come down uniformly through Church history, based solely on the literal Virginal Conception of Christ in the Matthean and Lukan genealogies.

John says Christ "became *flesh* and dwelt among us" (1:14). Though Jesus was sinless, John uses the crude word "flesh" (*egneto*) to stress the point that He was human. The influential French theologian John Calvin wrote:

> When it is said that the Word was made flesh, we must not understand it as if he were either changed into flesh, or confusedly intermingled with flesh, but that he made choice of the Virgin's womb as a temple in which he might dwell. He who was the Son of God became Son of man, not by confusion of substance, but by unity of person. For we maintain that the divinity was so conjoined and united with the humanity that the entire properties of each nature remain entire, and yet the two natures constitute only one Christ.[29]

The Christian teaching of the incarnation articulates that Jesus Christ (Second Person of the Trinity) is the Eternal Word who took on humanity (second nature) without diminishing His divine nature as God.

The ancient Church father, Saint Athanasius (ca. 296–373), in his remarkable writings, *The Incarnation of the Word of God*, sec. 17, penned these words,

The Word was not hedged in by His body, nor did His presence in the body prevent His being present elsewhere as well . . . at one and the same time—this is the wonder—as Man He was living a human life, and as Word He was sustaining the life of the Universe, and as Son He was in constant union with the Father.[30]

As Saint Athanasius indicated, Jesus's two natures did not mix, but worked in perfect unison, expressing all their own unique qualities with absolute consistency and revelation.

After years of rigorous theological debate among Church fathers and bishops over Christ's dual natures, the Council of Chalcedon (AD 451) produced a doctrinally sound creed to counter the heretical attacks of Nestorianism and Eutychianism. Its careful wording translated Scripture consistently and clarified the fact that Jesus was both fully human and fully divine.

Although the Chalcedon creed is a challenging text, it applies and defends the term *homoousios* ("being the same as God") to Jesus, not *homoiousios* ("to be like God"). Progressive Christians embrace *homoiousios*—meaning Jesus is "a good" person who reflected God-consciousness in the world. Biblical Christians, on the other hand, believe in *homoousios*—that Jesus is, as the Scriptures say, the perfect "image of the invisible God" (Colossians 1:15).

Many progressive Christians object, saying it is impossible to have both infinite and finite natures simultaneously, but there are several theological reasons we can embrace Christ's "hypostatic union."

For one, it is the *person* of Jesus Christ that is theanthropic, not His *nature*—meaning the God-man (fully God and fully man) is made up of the person of Jesus Christ, not the sum of His parts. Through the incarnation, the two natures were inseparably joined.

Second, in the incarnation, Jesus added a new manifestation of humanity but preserved His eternal divinity without change or defect. At this point, Jesus had two unique natures comprised of infinite and finite faculties which are separately expressed yet harmonious in the one Person.

Scripture shows us that Jesus's infinitely divine intelligence wasn't mixed with or transferred into His finitely human intelligence, as witnessed in the Garden of Gethsemane (Matthew 26:42). For example, Jesus says out of His divine nature that He was born before Abraham (John 8:58)—but proclaims through His finite nature that He is sometimes tired or hungry (John 4:6; Mark 11:12). Though both natures are simultaneously active in the person of Jesus Christ, they nonetheless consistently exist within their own identities.

Therefore, Jesus Christ retained the total complexity of divine and human attributes to exist as a perfect human being, and who is now and forever will be composed in this perfect body as the God-man.

Spiritual Results of Progressive Christianity

So what spiritual significance does the incarnation have to progressive Christianity?

According to Iliff School of Theology professor Delwin Brown, the "incarnation" isn't wrapped up in a single person or event but represents the divine virtues harmonizing in the natural world. Brown states, "The divine is at one with the cosmos and all that is in it. God is in and with the world. God is with us and the rest of creation, too—fully God, fully world, fully one."[31]

God incarnates (that is, involves) Himself in the affairs of the world to liberate His afflicted and oppressed children. In *Christianity in Blue*, David Kaden defines Jesus's birth and life on Earth as the incarnation of love "flowing through the world by the power of the Spirit of love."[32]

Therefore, we are to follow the love embodied in Jesus and seek to "incarnate" or produce divine blessings everyday as we do good deeds and overcome despair with hope.

Spiritual Results of Biblical Christianity

Richard Baxter brings to light the glorious gift of Jesus Christ coming to Earth and taking on flesh with these profound words:

> It was the greatest miracle of all God's works that ever He revealed to the sons of men, to take the human nature into union with the divine—that Christ, who was God, should condescend to be made man. And the next is that He will take His church into union with Himself, and will magnify His love, in such a wonderful advancement of poor sinners, that without His grace they could not well believe it.[33]

The incarnation reveals many things to us: It reveals God's love for us. It demonstrates what true love is. It provides a ransom for our sins (Hebrews 10:1–10). And someday, it means we will receive our resurrected bodies and dwell in Heaven with our Savior and Lord in blissful rest for eternity and beyond.

Key Points to Use When Talking to Progressive Christians

As antisupernaturalists, progressive Christians improperly exegete biblical texts to refute the virgin birth narrative. So, when talking about the Virginal Conception, keep in mind these four truths:

TELLING THE TWO APART

Progressive
Christianity (VS) Biblical
Christianity

Progressive Christians have different perspectives on the virgin birth, but generally claim Jesus did not miraculously come into the world. Either the disciples took ideas from pagan stories of virgin births, or the virgin story was later fused into the narrative to cover up a sex scandal between Mary and an older Roman soldier.	Biblical Christianity holds that the Virginal Conception shows Jesus's humanity by being born of a woman (Galatians 4:4–5) and His divinity through the power of the Spirit.

- **Historical:** Biblical Christians are not biased but are in fact the ones relying on early and accurate accounts that verify specific details surrounding the virgin birth story. Early Church fathers including Melito, Ignatius, Justin Martyr, Irenaeus, Clement of Alexandria, Tertullian, and Origen all embraced the Virginal Conception.

- **Biblical:** The Hebrew word *almah* and the Greek word *parthenos* plainly and emphatically describe Mary as a virgin who conceived Jesus through the power of the Holy Spirit.

- **Theological:** Progressive Christians assume Jews cherry-picked stories from paganism to make Jesus seem more divine. But the evidence shows that the "copycat conspiracies" and "scandalous cover-ups" have no factual, historical, or exegetical basis. In the incarnation, Jesus added a new manifestation of humanity but preserved His eternal divinity without change or defect.

- **Spiritual:** Our only hope for salvation rests on Jesus taking on flesh to pay the price for sinful mankind. The Scriptures openly state that He shared our "humanity" (Hebrews 2:14) and was "tempted" like us yet was without sin (Hebrews 4:15).

CHAPTER 5

Hijacking Jesus's
Miracles

F amed progressive writer Rachel Held Evans (1981–2019) often said that Christians should be less concerned with the historical authenticity of Jesus's miracles than with their spiritual significance—and many on both sides of the divide agree with her.[1]

However, despite Evans's personal affirmations of Jesus's resurrection, what her comments imply—and what other progressive Christians really mean—is that the Bible's stories about miracles are not actually true. They mean Christians get so caught up in verifying miracles that they lose sight of the everyday beauty of life. They say sharing happiness with someone, breathing in the fresh air, or performing an act of kindness all carry spiritual meaning and capture the miracle of life. And that's how they work to undermine the supernatural power Jesus displayed on Earth.

Historical Inquiries of Progressive Christianity

Previously, I highlighted a few key philosophers during the Rationalism and Enlightenment periods. One of the best known was David Hume (1711–1776), the "Father of Skepticism."

Unlike Benedict Spinoza (a rationalist who argued that miracles are simply impossible), Hume argued against miracles from an empirical perspective. For him, miracles are not impossible; they are incredible (cannot be empirically verified). He believed that since there is no real epistemological notion of the reality of God, then the conceptual meaning of God is nonsensical.

Hume argued that one either has relational ideas or matters of fact. Relational ideas are sensory customs, and matters of fact stem from causes and effects that lie beyond the sensory experience. One cannot know causal connections between things, he surmised; one can only believe in them based on customary conjunctions.

In his "Essay on Miracles" (1748), Hume denied the credibility of miracles because they are rare and often lack eyewitness testimony. Of course, that is because Hume did not consider any eyewitness accounts of the miracles reported in the Bible to be credible. After all, to him, the Bible itself is not credible.

On the other hand, Spinoza (1632–1677) asserted that the laws of nature cannot change—yet by definition, miracles do just that. Therefore, he said, miracles violate natural laws. For this reason, we should not be surprised that modern critics of the New Testament (who were heavily influenced by Hume and Spinoza) reject the miracles recorded in the gospels.

Paula Fredriksen is one such New Testament scholar.

To provide context to Jesus's miracles, she leans on pagan traditions and Jewish writings. She believes the gospel writers mimicked ancient stories to establish Jesus as a divine miracle worker.

Ancients would "incubate"—that is, sleep in at a cult site—in order to receive visions of or favors from a god. We have evidence of this practice from the cult of Asclepius, the god of healing. His worshipers, receiving cures, left a record of his miracles in inscriptions around his shrine. So also the pagan holy man Apollonius of Tyana had numerous miracles attributed to him: spectacular healings, exorcisms, even once raising someone from the dead. And in the Greek Magical Papyri—books for professionals consulted for cures and different kinds of help (in love or in betting on races, for example)—we can read recipes for conjuring demonic aid to achieve some of these ends. If these practices were not thought to be effective, if the miraculous and the wonderful were thought not to happen, we would not have so much ancient evidence that they did. Biblical and extrabiblical tradition, on the Jewish side, also speak of powerful prayer, miraculous cures, signs, and wonders.[2]

A post published on ProgressiveChristianity.org similarly states that people commonly believed in "miracles" (or superstition) when Jesus came on the scene; therefore, they weren't original to His public ministry.[3]

For progressive Christians, it boils down to three main points.

- Ancient people presumed miracles were common and therefore lack the ability to authenticate divine authority.
- Even if we could determine that Jesus was a "wonder worker," it wouldn't authenticate Him as God because miracles were imputed to other contemporaries, too.[4]

- The miracles Jesus allegedly performed were not as extreme as the gospel accounts indicate. At the very least, Jesus had a unique ability to help awaken people from comas but certainly not to miraculously raise them from the dead.

Historical Inquiries of Biblical Christianity

Progressive Christians correctly state that there are reports of ancient religious leaders allegedly performing supernatural feats. But contrary to popular belief, miracle workers were not commonplace in the ancient world.

There are records of Hellenistic miracle workers (or magicians) allegedly performing miracles, but these were later shown to be trickery.[5]

But Jesus's divine acts were different.

For his two-volume work *Miracles: The Credibility of the New Testament Accounts*, Craig Keener exhaustively researched the early stories and beliefs of miracles, listing several prominent progressive scholars who concede that Jesus's public ministry contained supernatural activities.

For instance, the late E. P. Sanders attests to the historical facts that Jesus healed people. He may not know how Jesus did it, but he acknowledges the "miracle stories" to be extraordinary accounts of Jesus that set Him apart from other teachers. Similarly, the late John Meier, another highly regarded scholar and Roman Catholic priest, did not dispute that miracles are extraordinarily attached to Jesus's ministry.

Even Morton Smith, among the recent scholars most
skeptical toward the Gospel tradition, argues that miracle
working is the most authentic part of the Jesus tradition,
though he explains it along the magical lines urged by
Jesus's early detractors.[6]

The liberal scholar Rudolf Bultmann states that Jesus really
"healed the sick and expelled demons."[7] He does not explain by what
means Jesus did such extraordinary deeds but acknowledges that
Jesus's ministry included "supernatural" activity.

Clearly, even some of the most liberal and progressive scholars
acknowledge that Jesus was a miracle worker. However, that is not
to say they believed in the nature of miracles recorded in the Bible.
The progressive viewpoint on that aspect of His being seems to have
begun early in the twentieth century, when influential scholars began
to interpret the "miracle stories" of Jesus to be equivalent to magical
stories in the Greco-Roman world.

Richard Horsley, formerly a professor at the University of
Massachusetts–Boston, presents their faulty interpretation by stating, "A
bold and wide-ranging argument that Jesus was a magician was based on
uncritical readings of both Gospel narratives and passages in the 'magical
papyri.'"[8] He notes that modern biblical scholarship improperly interprets
the use of "miracles" in ancient times through an antisupernaturalistic
lens inspired by the Enlightenment. This creates substantial problems,
because bringing in a modern definition of "miracles" completely strips
the literary context of the "miracle stories" of Jesus

William Wrede (1859–1906) admitted in *The Skeptical Critique*
that liberal scholars were not objective in their analysis of the Synoptic
Gospels. They simply excluded whatever they felt was not true to the

traditions of the early writers. Rather, Wrede argued, the Gospel narratives are theologically constructed and therefore are meant to be treated as literature, not merely historical documents.

S. Vernon McCasland, in his classic piece, "Signs and Wonders," published in *The Society of Biblical Literature and Exegesis* (1957), persuasively argues believing in the supernatural was not a sign of fatuousness among ancient near-Eastern and Greek societies—quite the opposite. Ancient near-Eastern people, including the Greeks, did not see miracles as contradictions in the natural realm. They believed they came from a supernatural source outside their realm to present divine signs.[9]

There is ample early documentation of Jesus's miracles.

- The Gospels (including "Q") are early first-century accounts of Jesus that contain stories of Him working miracles.
- Josephus describes Jesus as a "doer of startling deeds" (*Antiquities* 18:63).
- The Babylonian Talmud (Sanhedrin 107B) claims Jesus deceived the Jews with his magic: "Yeshu stood up a brick to symbolize an idol and bowed down to it. Jesus performed magic and incited the people of Israel and led them astray."
- Even the second-century Church critic Celsus acknowledges that Jesus performed miracles—although he calls it sorcery.

Another significant validation of the historicity of Jesus's miracles comes from Denver Seminary professor Craig Blomberg.

In short, the nature miracles and the parables closely cohere with each other. . . . It therefore follows that the earliest forms of these miracle stories should be recognized as most probably historical.[10]

A thorough and objective examination of the parallels between Jesus's parables and miracles leads one to conclude that the stories and their associated beliefs were foundational to Christianity. This is an extremely important argument because Jesus's teachings are widely recognized as authentic, lending credibility to His miracles.

Biblical Explanations of Progressive Christianity

Against the background of rationalism, the German theologian H. E. G. Paulus treated Jesus's miracles not as divine acts, but simply as mistakes: Jesus walking on water was nothing more than an optical illusion from the disciples' vantage point.[11]

David F. Strauss claims the disciples were not fooled into believing Jesus performed extraordinary deeds, such as raising the dead or rising from the dead Himself. Instead, Strauss argues the disciples' frame of reference was not as an eyewitness of actual events of the miraculous, but one that originated from myth or sacred legend.[12] According to Bishop John Shelby Spong, Jesus's miracles cannot be true because science proves miracles do not happen. Spong goes so far as to suggest that people who believe they did happen are gullible.[13] He tries to discredit the Bible's miracles by claiming the four gospels contradict each other:

One needs to know that Mark and Matthew say this miraculous feeding episode actually happened twice in two different locations with a different number of people, a different number of loaves and a different amount of left-overs (Mark 6:30–44, 8:1–10, Matt. 14:13–21, 15:32–39). Does that make two miracles? Luke and John, however, disagree with Mark and Matthew and say that a miraculous feeding of the multitude happened only once (Luke 9:10–17, John 6:1–14). Even then there is still confusion, since John places the event early in the ministry of Jesus in Jerusalem and at the Passover (6:4).[14]

Later Spong concludes that a "literal supernatural reading of the gospels would be a violation of the original intent of the gospel writers."[15] He rationalizes that Jesus

did not walk on water, heal the sick, or raise the dead. Rather, in his radical humanity, he lived out the meaning of God and caused those who glimpsed his life or felt his power to exclaim, "God was in Christ," and thus God, the gospel writers assert, can also be in you and in me.[16]

In one of his most complex works, *The Historical Christ and the Theological Jesus*, Dale Allison asks:

How can anyone with a good education wholeheartedly believe that Jesus walked on water, that he fed five thousand with a few food scraps, or that he restored the dead to the land of the living? Such incredible things seem opposed to ordinary human experience. Similar things do, however, often appear in archaic tales that everybody knows to be fictional—the apocryphal gospels, for instance—tales that once fed what appears to have been an insatiable craving for the marvelous. It is no mystery why Reimarus, Strauss, and Bultmann regarded the miracle stories of the Gospels as pious fictions. They were just being reasonable—and treating the Gospels the same way that the rest of us treat the fantastic fables of the Greek gods. One understands the modern habit of preferring, on principle, natural causes to miraculous causes.[17]

A post on ProgressiveChristianity.org titled "Affirmations and Confessions by a Progressive Christian Layman—Jesus' Miracles" analyzes the various miracles recorded in the four gospels. The blogger concludes they must only be understood metaphorically.

For instance, in the healing of the paralyzed man (Mark 2:1–12; Luke 5:17–26), the blogger questions the legitimacy of the miracle by asking, "Isn't it possible that this miracle is about a person who was spiritually paralyzed rather than physically paralyzed?"[18]

Elsewhere, utilizing a modern interpretation of the healing of the blind man caused by a demon, the blogger notes, "In the twenty-first century we know that not being able to see or speak has nothing to do with demon possession. These are medical conditions that cannot be cured by an exorcism."[19]

Fredriksen offers a more conservative interpretation. Although she believes the miracle accounts are mostly considered legends, she does apply a level of confidence to Jesus's miracle-working power.

> [Jesus] probably did work miracles and exorcisms. For one thing, he had a popular following, which an ability to work cures would account for (Mk 1:23–28, 32, 39). Such abilities, in an age of so many healers and miracle-workers, would confer no unique distinction upon Jesus; but coupled with his moral message and his call to prepare for the Kingdom, they may have enhanced his reputation as an authoritative prophet.[20]

Biblical Explanations of
Biblical Christianity

The historic Christian faith wholeheartedly believes, affirms, and confesses that Jesus is God and that His miracles were literal events. The idea that Jesus used trickery or incantations to put spells on people to make it look as if He healed them is ludicrous.[21] A straightforward reading of Jesus's miracles reveals that He did not use incantations, sorcery, or potions to generate partial healings.

N. T. Wright says Jesus's miracles

> indicate, rather, that something has happened, *within* what we would call the "natural" world, which is not what would have been anticipated, and which seems to provide evidence for the active presence of an authority, a power, at work, not invading the created order as an alien force, but rather enabling it to be more truly itself.[22]

It should be noted that first-century Jews, including Jesus's disciples, were not gullible about the supernatural. They were well acquainted with miracles. Even in the Roman imperial period, people were able to tell the difference between miracles and magic: Magic is done by deception and cannot oppose or overpower God, whereas miracles can only be performed and controlled by God and, therefore, can overpower any kind of evil.

Jesus demonstrated His divine power and authority to perform miracles as He felt necessary.

The New Testament principally uses four Greek words to designate miracles:

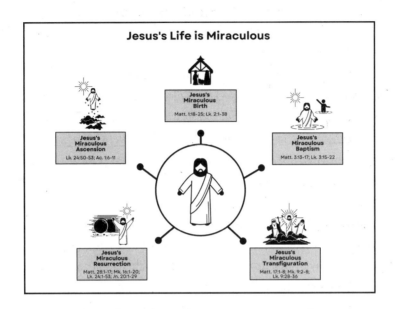

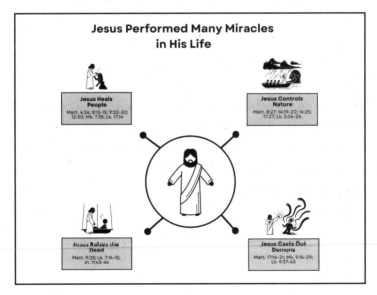

1. *Semeion*, a "sign,", i.e., an evidence of a divine commission; an attestation of a divine message (Matthew 12:38–39; 16:1, 4; Mark 8:11; Luke 11:16; 23:8; John 2:11, 18, 23; Acts 6:8, etc.); a token of the presence and working of God; the seal of a higher power.
2. *Terata*, "wonders," wonder-causing events; portents; producing astonishment in the beholder (Acts 2:19).
3. *Dunameis*, "mighty works," works of superhuman power (Acts 2:22; Romans 15:19; 2 Thessalonians 2:9); of a new and higher power.
4. *Erga*, "works," the works of Him who is "wonderful in working" (John 5:20, 36).[23]

Nelson's Introduction to the Christian Faith devotes a large section to explaining the purpose and meaning of Jesus's miracles.

It was not that Jesus went about looking for people to heal. The Gospels do not reflect a deliberate "healing campaign." But he had a power over both physical and spiritual evil, and a sympathy for those in need, which naturally moved him to heal those who came to him. And they came in vast numbers. So there is no doubt that one of the main impressions Jesus made on people was of a man of supernatural power—power which he used to meet human need, whether sickness, hunger, or danger. No wonder people started asking who he could be.[24]

If Jesus's miracles were nothing more than magical spells, it would mean He was a fraud. However, we do not worship some disillusioned sorcerer who fooled people into believing He had divine powers. The

Jesus we worship is a wonder-working God who touched lives on Earth with His heavenly power, restored people to life, and still performs miracles today.

Jesus is our incredible, miracle-working Savior!

Theological Arguments of Progressive Christianity

Progressive Christians categorically reject miracles in the space-time continuum.

The theological giant, Rudolph Bultmann, was the first to propose "demythologizing" biblical miracles:

> Experience and control of the world have developed to such an extent through science and technology that no one can or does seriously maintain the New Testament world picture. What sense does it make to confess today "he descended into hell" or "he ascended into heaven," if the confessor no longer shares the underlying mythical world picture of a three-story world?[25]

In *Jesus for the Non-Religious*, Spong conveys his aversion to miracles and dismay that people still believe in them.

> I do not . . . believe in a deity who does miracles—nor do I even want such a God. I do not wish to live in a world in which an intervening deity acts capriciously to accomplish the divine will by overriding the laws of nature established in creation. The problems posed by the miracle stories historically associated with the life of Jesus are thus for me something that I must be able to view differently than traditional Christians do.[26]

Scotty McLennan, a self-identifying Christian liberal, follows the same reasoning, writing,

> What's not religious or what belittles the creation and its order for me is the claim that every so often a Supreme Being breaks in and violates the natural order of the universe for this or that reason (say, suspending gravity or reversing it so that someone who's jumped out a skyscraper window flies back in, or reversing time so that an accident that's already occurred never happened).[27]

McLennan adamantly protests the factuality of miracles on two fronts: One, they are only religious or spiritual judgments; and two, they detract from the awe of natural order. Taking a cue from the atheist Richard Dawkin's *The God Delusion*, McLennan says the natural laws that govern the universe are magnificent in their own right and therefore, God doesn't have to use miracles to impress us.[28]

Diana Butler, in remarking on Mark 1:34 (which reads, "And [Jesus] healed many who were sick with various diseases, and cast out many demons."), claims Jesus did use the same practices as other miracle workers, healers, and exorcists, so these miracles did not confirm His identity as Messiah; they were simply ways Jesus was bringing healing and wholeness to a broken world.

Sarah Bessey, cofounder and cohost of the progressive Evolving Faith Conference and podcast, describes miracles as an "act of protest, a snatching back from darkness, a proclamation of freedom, a revolution of love."[29]

Theological Arguments of Biblical Christianity

The naturalism that financed Hume's rejection of miracles was fraught with fallacies. Hume, an empiricist, prejudicially puts together a straw man for miracles, believing he's disproven them. In his book *Miracles: The Credibility of the New Testament Accounts*, Craig Keener writes,

> Hume manages to define away any possibility of a miracle occurring, by defining "miracle" as a violation of natural law, yet defining "natural law" as principles that cannot be violated."[30]

However, there is some bad news for Hume and the progressive Christians who adopt his line of thinking.

Miracles Are Rare

Hume gets the definition of miracles all wrong. Miracles are rare or irregularities. They do not happen all the time. Otherwise, they would not stand out from the norm in any way. We can predict common or regular natural occurrences based on their physical conditions—but not miracles.

Differences between Natural and Supernatural Events	
Natural Occurrences	Supernatural Occurrences
Regular	Irregular
Repeatable	Not Repeatable
Predictable	Not Predictable

Modifying the definition of "miracle" as a special act of God that is an exception to the general rule moves miracles from impossible to possible. Hume never shut the door on the possibility of miracles; he left it wide open.

Miracles Do Not Violate the Laws of Nature

If God exists and created all the other things that now exist—which includes the laws of nature[31]—then it is safe to assume He is not restricted by any of them. When God intervenes in nature, He sometimes suspends the laws for a greater purpose. As C. S. Lewis said, if Nature was, "left to her own resources, she could never produce them."[32]

Therefore, if a miracle is not altering physics or violating other laws of nature, it follows that natural law does not conflict with the miraculous.

Science Cannot Test Miracles

Hume rejects the supernatural on the basis that there is no evidence for it. By definition, miracles are performed by a metaphysical/transcendent deity (i.e., God) making Himself immanent in the physical realm.[33] Therefore, how can Hume know the supernatural does not exist if science (which is limited to nature) cannot "test" that which is "beyond" the natural realm?

Miracles Are Historically Verifiable

Hume also claims miracles are not historically verifiable: If you cannot test it in a lab, then you cannot trust it. But miracles do not lie outside the purview of historical inquiry. While historians may not be able to explain how things occurred, they certainly can accurately report that they happened. And the collective facts of history point to Jesus as a public first-century figure who had the power to perform miracles.

Difference between God's General and Special Providence

Former pastor Rob Bell makes a weak argument against miracles when he writes,

> When people argue for the existence of a supernatural God who is somewhere else and reaches in on occasion to do a miracle or two, they're skipping over the very world that surrounds us and courses through our veins and lights up the sky right here, right now.[34]

Notice the non sequitur.

Bell mistakenly believes God is distant from His creation. He also confuses God's general providence with His special acts. General providence refers to the care and sustaining power God exhibits in nature, including the rain and sun and even the fact that our hearts continue to beat. Special providence is just that: unique and specific.

The same God who actively created the universe is the same God who came into the world and performed miracles. And yet, with all the complexity, specificity, and harmonious regularity of the universe, progressive Christians quickly deny that God can perform special acts in nature.

Jesus's Miracles Prove He Is the Messiah

What do the gospels actually teach us about the miracles Jesus performed?

Let's examine one specific account: when Jesus took the loaves and the fish and gave thanks to God, and the food miraculously multiplied to feed more than five thousand people.

What did the crowd think of that miracle?

After the people had eaten and were full, they realized what Jesus had done in their presence and said, "This is indeed the Prophet who is to come into the world" (John 6:14). The crowd alluded to Jesus being a "prophet" who comes in the spirit of Moses (Deuteronomy 18:15). Doing this showed they deemed Him to be more significant than Moses, Elijah, and John the Baptist!

The graph below highlights the various purposes of Jesus's miracles:

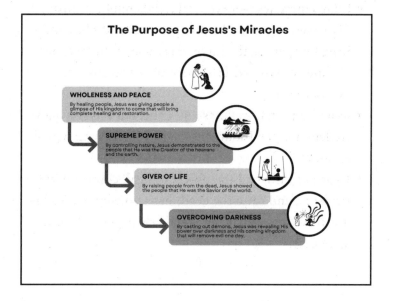

The Purpose of Jesus's Miracles

WHOLENESS AND PEACE
By healing people, Jesus was giving people a glimpse of His kingdom to come that will bring complete healing and restoration.

SUPREME POWER
By controlling nature, Jesus demonstrated to the people that He was the Creator of the heavens and the earth.

GIVER OF LIFE
By raising people from the dead, Jesus showed the people that He was the Savior of the world.

OVERCOMING DARKNESS
By casting out demons, Jesus was revealing His power over darkness and His coming kingdom that will remove evil one day.

Here are seven other facts to consider:

- Jesus's miracles were not isolated incidents. Many of them were public, and many crowds called Him a "miracle worker" (Matthew 12:38–39).
- The records of Jesus's miracles are accompanied by eyewitness testimony and personal accounts from some of the people He healed (Mark 1:32–34, 45; 2:1–2, 13; 3:7–12).

- Jesus's opponents examined His miracles and verified them to be acts of God—to the point that the religious leaders believed His powers came from Beelzebub and eventually sought to have Him killed.
- Jesus's miracles were not restricted to people and their ailments. He also had power over storms, turned water into wine, walked on water, predicted finding money in a fish, and withered a fig tree overnight with a curse.
- Jesus's miracles were central to His public ministry.[35] They were signs of His divine power and His coming Kingdom on Earth (Luke 7:22; 10:13). In fact, being a healer enhanced His work as a traveling teacher (Mark 9:28).
- Jesus's supernatural acts authenticated His Messianic credentials (see Isaiah 9:6–7; 11:3–5; 32:3–4; 35:5–6; 61:1–2).
- Jesus not only had the power to heal, control natural elements, and raise the dead, but also empowered His disciples to cast out demons and heal people (Mark 1:15; 5:30; 9:38).

Spiritual Results of Progressive Christianity

For progressive Christians, the factual truth about whether Jesus healed people is not important as whether we love people the way He showed us to.

For David Kaden, the UCC minister mentioned previously in these pages, the miracle in Mark 1:40–42 was not that Jesus healed a man of leprosy, but that He touched him despite the fact that Jewish culture forbade Him from doing so.

The way Kaden sees it, Jesus was breaking down the social taboos to show us how to embrace people for who they are and what they believe.

> This story begs to be applied in our day, when so many of our LGBTQ+ siblings feel barred from entering churches. They aren't lepers but have been made to feel like lepers. And because of the irrational fears of many non-Muslims, our Muslim siblings, too, have been made to feel marginal—a marginality concretized in travel bans and hate crimes. . . . If Jesus was moved with pity—if his guts ached for outsiders—enough to cross a rigid border and perform a touching miracle, surely we, his followers, can touch and even embrace those who have been made to feel marginal in our world.[36]

Progressive pastor John Pavlovitz captures the spiritual reality of the Divine by stating,

> Despite our religious worldview or our practiced theology, we can all recognize a kind of sacredness in the disparate experiences of this life: standing in a crowd singing along to a band we love or hiking alone through a sunlit mountain pass or tasting food so delicious that it generates an involuntary sound of gastronomic adoration from somewhere deep within us. . . . [the miraculous is the] breathtaking stuff of butterflies and goose bumps.[37]

Spiritual Results of Biblical Christianity

The facts that God created the heavens and the earth and also sent His Son to forgive you of your sins are incredible miracles that should not be taken for granted.

Once you understand that the universe is set in order by a Creator, then it is possible to believe that things like parting the Red Sea, turning water into wine, and Jesus rising from the dead are all things the Creator could easily do.

In *Miracles*, C. S. Lewis wrote that objections to miracles are often based on the suspicion that the characters are in some kind of difficulty from which they need to be rescued, and the rescuing event did not really belong to that story.

Miracles are not of this class. They are essential to the central theme in His-story.

God is purposefully working out His plans and actively working in our lives through both miracles and general providence.

Whether it is to bring peace to our land, restore a broken marriage, or heal a person from cancer, we believe God has both the power and the compassion to perform miracles.

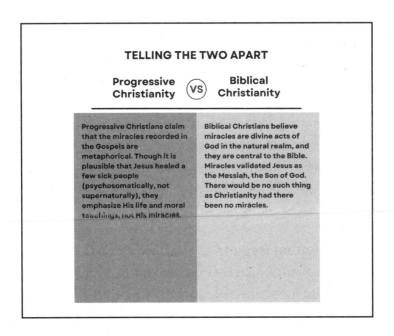

TELLING THE TWO APART

Progressive Christianity (VS) **Biblical Christianity**

Progressive Christians claim that the miracles recorded in the Gospels are metaphorical. Though it is plausible that Jesus healed a few sick people (psychosomatically, not supernaturally), they emphasize His life and moral teachings, not His miracles.

Biblical Christians believe miracles are divine acts of God in the natural realm, and they are central to the Bible. Miracles validated Jesus as the Messiah, the Son of God. There would be no such thing as Christianity had there been no miracles.

Key Points to Use When Talking
to Progressive Christians

A hallmark of progressive Christianity is rejecting the supernatural events recorded in the canonical gospels and denying the miraculous claims of Jesus. Therefore, keep these points in mind when discussing miracles with progressive Christians.

- **Historical:** In addition to the canonical gospels, early extrabiblical sources cite Jesus as a miracle worker. Furthermore, most scholars accept the fact that Jesus's ministry consisted of performing "supernatural acts" or "wonders."
- **Biblical:** There is no evidence that Jesus was a sorcerer who performed magic tricks; that would make Him a deceiver. The canonical gospels record nearly forty miracles Jesus performed, indicating most of them were observed in public.
- **Theological:** A miracle is a special act of God, a rare event that suspends (but does not violate) the laws of nature for a greater purpose.
- **Spiritual:** Miracles are not hard to accept when considering that the greatest one occurred when God created the universe (Genesis 1:1; Job 26:10; Psalm 33:6; Jeremiah 10:12).

CHAPTER 6

Hijacking Jesus's

Atonement

COVID-19 caused millions of deaths, shut down the economy, and disrupted billions of lives worldwide. But to some progressive Christians, the doctrine of atonement has done—and will continue to do—far worse things. Dawn Hutchings, who pastors a Lutheran congregation in Canada, recently wrote:

> Now is the time to vaccinate ourselves against the virus of atonement theology, which threatens to afflict our vision and restrict our ability to see Jesus . . . before we are blinded by proclamations of blood-sacrifice, let us vaccinate ourselves, lest the infection of atonement theology force us to look away from the realities of Jesus' life and death, in favour of the blood-soaked wet dream of a god which is unworthy of our worship![1]

Shocking as that is, Hutchings's train of thought has long roots through the last century. Many liberal and progressive thinkers including Thomas Priestly, William Ellery Channing, Ralph Waldo Emerson, and Richard Rohr have advanced a dangerous doctrine proclaiming that Jesus didn't believe in or teach that there was such a thing as original sin.

Boston University religion professor Stephen Prothero says many liberal Protestants affirmed Jesus's divinity of Jesus but began to emphasize some of His features over others.

> They emphasized his birth instead of his resurrection, the incarnation rather than the atonement, his immanence rather than his transcendence. More a moralist than a miracle worker, their Jesus came to earth not to satisfy a legal judgment or to pay a debt owed to an angry Father but to reveal to human beings the loving character of God, and to prompt them to develop that same character in themselves. His death saved sinners not from hell (which few liberals believed in anymore) but from selfish solitude. The new birth he offered was essentially moral, an awakening to a life of sympathy with all of God's children.[2]

Most progressive Christians believe the doctrine of atonement is a horrific theology that has tainted Christianity, and Borg goes so far as to consider believing in it to be "precritical naiveté."[3]

Historical Inquiries of Progressive Christianity

Several progressive thinkers offer different views as to how the doctrine of atonement became a staple in Christianity. An article posted on Beliefnet.com, titled "Jesus Did Not Die on the Cross for Our Sins," explains atonement this way:

> No matter how hard you search, you will not find a single passage in the entire Bible that says anything about Jesus paying the penalty for our sins. That's because this is a "Christian belief" that the Bible doesn't teach. Rather it was a theology created by humans.
>
> The technical, theological name for this belief is "penal substitutionary atonement." This theology was not part of Christian doctrine for the first 1,600 years after Jesus was crucified. The idea was originated and developed by human beings who were having trouble understanding what the Bible teaches about how Jesus Christ saved humanity. They worked with what they could to better understand Jesus' teachings, but missed the mark. This lead (sic) to a creation of a belief that wasn't really based on the Bible.[4]

Likewise, Marcus J. Borg discusses the term "atonement" in church history.

> [The] first systematic articulation of the cross as "payment for sin" happened just over nine hundred years ago in 1098 in St. Anselm's treatise *Cur Deus Homo?* [*Why Did God Become Human?*] Anselm's purpose was to provide a rational argument for the necessity of the incarnation and death of Jesus . . . Anselm then applied that model to our relationship with God.[5]

The progressive evangelical pastor and activist Doug Pagitt claims the Christian idea of atonement developed in this way:

[T]he early evangelists recognized they could help the Jesus story make sense if Jesus was seen as someone who was chosen to appease the wrath of God—hence, the "anointed one" who could do what no one else could do.[6]

Progressives say six key moments in history shifted Christians' thinking on the meaning of Jesus's death.

- Personal commitment to Jesus as "Savior" crept in through early disciples, who began formulating teachings about His death and resurrection.
- Early Christians refused to accept much of Judaism and eventually separated around AD 88, causing many more Christians to become antisemitic.
- Christian theology developed under the guise and influence of Neoplatonic philosophy.
- As time went on, more dogma gained traction, particularly the doctrines of the incarnation, atonement, and the Trinity.
- By the fourth century, Constantine had made Christianity the official religion of the Roman empire, pushing a politicized version that stripped away the timely truths of Jesus and His teachings.
- Many "traditional symbols" were erected, tainting Jesus's Jewishness by making Him into a deified Savior who atoned for the sins of the world.

Historical Inquiries of Biblical Christianity

The term "at-one-ment" ("making at one" or "making amends") is an Anglo-Saxon term put into use long after the Bible was canonized.

The concept can be traced to Anselm's work, *Cur Deus Homo* ("Why God Became Man") in the eleventh century, but not until William Tyndale was translating the Bible into English in 1526 did it become a word. Tyndale created "at-one-ment" (derived from the adverbial phrase *atonen*, "in accord," literally, at one[7]) to capture the meaning of "reconciliation."

Though the word, "at-one-ment," does not appear in the New Testament, the concept and imagery of atonement are implied.

In keeping with the Hebrews' exodus from Egypt (Exodus 15:1–21), the first-century Christians reckoned that Jesus was the Passover Lamb who was killed on their behalf, delivering them from sin and death.[8]

Although the canonical gospels are not theological treatises, they portray Jesus's death on the cross as the fulfillment of Passover. In the book of Acts, we see not a doctrinal discourse of the atonement but an affirmation of what Christ's death meant to first-century Christians. Peter declared on the Day of Pentecost (fifty days after Jesus's resurrection):

> [T]his Jesus, delivered up according to the definite plan
> and foreknowledge of God, you crucified and killed by
> the hands of lawless men. God raised him up, loosing the
> pangs of death, because it was not possible for him to be
> held by it. (Acts 2:23–24)

Peter then immediately tells the audience to "Repent and be baptized every one of you in the name of Jesus Christ for the forgiveness of your sins" (Acts 2:38—clearly indicating he believed the gospel of Jesus's death and resurrection to be inextricably linked to atonement.)[9]

A few years later, in the early 50s, Paul explains to the Corinthians one of the reasons Jesus died on the cross:

For I delivered to you as of first importance what I also received: that Christ *died for our sins* in accordance with the Scriptures. (1 Corinthians 15:3; emphasis added)

To demonstrate Jesus's victory, the early Christians created symbols to discreetly communicate with each other. The fish symbol *icthys* was an acronym for *Iesus Christos Theou Huios Sotēr*, translated as "Jesus Christ, the Son of God, Savior." Other symbols included the ark of Noah, Abraham sacrificing the ram in place of Isaac, and Daniel in the lion's den. But each image represented the Church's belief that Jesus's death was a sacrifice for their sins. By the turn of the second century, the universally accepted symbol of Christianity was the cross.[10]

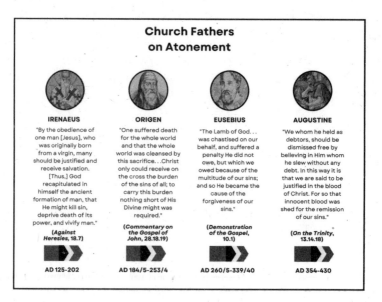

Church Fathers on Atonement

IRENAEUS

"By the obedience of one man [Jesus], who was originally born from a virgin, many should be justified and receive salvation. [Thus,] God recapitulated in himself the ancient formation of man, that He might kill sin, deprive death of its power, and vivify man."

(Against Heresies, 18.7)

AD 125-202

ORIGEN

"One suffered death for the whole world and that the whole world was cleansed by this sacrifice. . .Christ only could receive on the cross the burden of the sins of all; to carry this burden nothing short of His Divine might was required."

(Commentary on the Gospel of John, 28.18.19)

AD 184/5-253/4

EUSEBIUS

"The Lamb of God. . . was chastised on our behalf, and suffered a penalty He did not owe, but which we owed because of the multitude of our sins; and so He became the cause of the forgiveness of our sins."

(Demonstration of the Gospel, 10.1)

AD 260/5-339/40

AUGUSTINE

"We whom he held as debtors, should be dismissed free by believing in Him whom he slew without any debt. In this way it is that we are said to be justified in the blood of Christ. For so that innocent blood was shed for the remission of our sins."

(On the Trinity, 13.14.18)

AD 354-430

As the faith expanded, many Church fathers debated the reason for Christ's death on the cross. Although there would be considerable disagreements about *how* atonement worked, it is quite clear that the

New Testament writers and early Church fathers believed in Jesus's victory over death. The graphic on the previous page highlights some views of prominent Church fathers on the extent of the death of Jesus Christ on the cross.

Biblical Explanations of Progressive Christianity

Progressive pastor and theologian Gregory Boyd of Minnesota, mentioned previously in this book, believes Western Christians are too fixated on Jesus's death as an act of propitiation on our behalf. Instead, Boyd sees Jesus's death and resurrection as Christ's cosmic victory over the world—a view known as "Christus Victor."

> The New Testament concept of salvation does not first and foremost mean "salvation from God's wrath" and/or "salvation from hell" as many western Christians take it to mean—often with negative consequences for their mental picture of God and/or antinomian consequences for their life. [11]

Bradley Jersak's book, *A More Christlike God: A More Beautiful Gospel,* is a comprehensive look at the doctrine of atonement throughout Church history. Jersak does not fully deny the atoning sacrifice of Jesus on the cross. He does, however, reject the idea of Jesus taking on the wrath of God on behalf of sinful humanity and dismisses the reality of an eternal hell.[12]

In his book *What Is the Bible?*, Rob Bell asks plainly, "Did Jesus have to die?" And then answers: "No. He didn't. He was killed.[13]

Bell also produced a DVD called *The Gods Aren't Angry* in which he flatly rejects the notion that Jesus's blood is necessary for salvation, suggesting that Jesus's death wasn't a sacrifice to atone for our sins but a selfless act to heal the world of oppression and violence.[14]

Bell's view of the atonement is framed by Peter Abelard's Moral-Influence theory (constructed in the early twelfth century), emphasizing that Jesus's death on the cross acted as a moral example for us to follow to reestablish a loving relationship with God.[15]

Biblical Explanations of Biblical Christianity

Since the Fall of Adam and Eve in the Garden of Eden (Genesis 3), a death penalty has been enforced on the rest of humanity.

However, God the Father, before the foundation of the world, ordained that He would send His Son, Jesus Christ, to save humanity through His death on the cross. Therefore, both the Old and New Testaments declare the doctrine of atonement loudly and clearly.

God promised to establish a great nation, Israel, from Abraham's bloodline (see Genesis 12:2–3; 18:17–19). More than nine hundred years later, He made another everlasting covenant with King David, promising that a Redeemer would come from one of his descendants to restore God's people to Him (see 2 Samuel 7; 1 Chronicles 17:11–14). The eighth-century prophet Isaiah (739–681 BC) foretold in very comprehensive terms the costly atonement of the coming Messiah who, through His sacrificial death, would forgive humanity's sins and bring healing and restoration (52:13–53:12) to their relationship with God.

In the first century, John the Baptist saw Jesus walking toward him and exclaimed, "Behold, the Lamb of God, who takes away the sin of the world!" (John 1:29).

Two years later, Jesus told His audience,

I am the good shepherd. The good shepherd lays down his life for the sheep. (John 10:11)

The Greek word Jesus uses for "lay down" or "die" is *hyper*, a word used throughout John's gospel that almost exclusively speaks to His sacrificial death on our behalf.

After a dispute broke out over which of the disciples was the greatest, Jesus reminded them of His ultimate purpose on Earth. It was not to establish a kingdom, but "to give his life as a ransom for many" (Mark 10:45).

The word "ransom" is *lytron* in Greek and can be used as a synonym for "expiation" or "propitiation"[16]—a clear sign Jesus was connecting Himself directly to the Suffering Servant mentioned in Isaiah 53:10–12.

A few months later, He created the new tradition of Communion ("the Lord's Supper") out of Passover meal[17] to highlight His role as the long-promised Redeemer and Deliverer and memorialize His death for coming generations.

Within twenty-five years of Jesus's resurrection, the Apostle Paul pieces together the works and effects of the atonement (Romans 5:6–10), mentioning that Christ "died for" (*apothnēskō hyper*) our sins four times. The preposition "for" (*hyper* or *huper*) means "to die for the sake of, on behalf of, instead of."[18] He lists three salvific truths resulting from the atoning sacrifice of Jesus.

- We have been "justified by his blood" (Greek, *dikaioō en autos haima*) (Romans 5:9). Most scholars believe Paul's use of "blood" is alluding to Leviticus 17:11, "For the life of the flesh is in the blood, and I have given it for you on the altar to make atonement for your souls, for it is the blood that makes atonement by the life." Contextually, Paul is pointing out that Jesus Christ (the "Lamb of God," John 1:29) is the fulfillment of the animal sacrifices traditionally given on Israel's behalf on the Day of Atonement (see 1 Peter 1:18–19; 2:22–25).

- We are "saved by him from the wrath of God." The word Paul chooses for "saved" is *sōzō*, "to save, to deliver." This matches what Jesus said in John 5:24: "Whoever hears my word and believes him who sent me has eternal life. He does not come into judgment, but has passed from death to life."
- We are "reconciled to God" (Romans 5:10). The very concept of reconciliation with a deity would have been shocking and foreign to the Greeks and Romans.

Based on Romans 5 alone, it is indisputable that Paul and the early Christians strongly believed and advanced the atonement of Christ as a sacrifice for humanity's sins; without it, there would be no possibility of forgiveness.

Theological Arguments of Progressive Christianity

Progressive Christians have various views of atonement, but the primary one is that the substitutionary atonement of Jesus is a despicable doctrine that eventually crept into Christianity.

Atonement Is a Cruel and Barbaric Doctrine

After publishing *The Shack* (and selling more than twenty million copies!), the popular novelist William Paul Young felt the need to write a nonfiction book about the lies we believe about God.

Young flat-out blasts atonement as a horrific way of viewing God. He rhetorically asks, "Who originated the Cross?" and then answers by stating:

If God did, then we worship a cosmic abuser, who in
Divine Wisdom created a means to torture human beings
in the most painful and abhorrent manner.[19]

One progressive blogger suggests atonement makes Jesus out to
be "a magical scapegoat."

The doctrine of substitutionary atonement states that
God requires payment for every sin we've ever committed.
In this context, the suffering and death of Jesus was the
payment for every sin committed by human beings. This
makes Jesus into a magical scapegoat and God into a book-
keeper who wants debts paid. . . . A deity that requires the
death of another to atone for grievances is simply cruel
and barbaric.[20]

In his study *Death of Jesus for Progressive Christians*, Donald
Schmidt claims the cross ignores Hosea 6:6, in which God declares
that He "desires faithful love and not sacrifice." And yet,

It seems odd . . . after having condemned the sacrificial cult
for several hundred years, God would demand a sacrifice
(in this case, nothing less than God's own son) on behalf
of the people.[21]

Lynda Serene Jones, president and Johnston Family Professor for
Religion and Democracy at Union Theological Seminary, openly
declares,

The pervasive idea of an abusive God-father who sends his
own kid to the cross so God could forgive people is nuts.[22]

Jesus Was Not a Substitution for Sin on Humanity's Behalf

Schmidt points out that Jesus's death on the cross implies that God is bound by rules.

> The idea that God would be bound by a rule—as if shrugging divine shoulders and saying, "Sorry, I wish someone didn't have to die, but my hands are tied"—presents us with an image of a rather "small" and ineffectual God.[23]

In repudiating the atonement of Jesus, Felten and Procter-Murphy quote the historic-process theologian John B. Cobbs, who stated,

> The atonement doctrine, which puts an emphasis on Jesus's blood as being the sacrifice, is really a mistranslation of Romans Chapter 3 where it simply means that Jesus's faithfulness to death is the saving factor.[24]

Likewise, Marcus Borg says "the language of sacrifice does not intrinsically mean substitution,"[25] and Richard Rohr believes Jesus came to save the world by turning "exponential revenge into exponential forgiveness."[26]

Then there's Tony Jones. Jones self-identifies as a progressive Christian who, unlike a whole host of others, happens to believe in Jesus's miracles and resurrection, and promotes the doctrinal affirmation of Jesus as God. Nevertheless, he does not believe in original sin or the penal substitutionary atonement of Jesus Christ. In *Did God Kill Jesus?: Searching for Love in History's Most Famous Execution*, Jones argues that Jesus's atonement has never risen to a level of theological orthodoxy by which we measure a person's salvation.[27] The cross, rather, is only a symbol of Jesus's love to free humanity from shame and guilt—not a symbol of Him as a necessary sacrifice to atone for the sins of humanity.

Thus, Jesus's death is how He identified with us and us with God.[28]

Theological Arguments of Biblical Christianity

At the heart of Christian thought lies the idea that sin entered the world and affected our perfect and complete relationship with God. Now, with sin natures, we are incapable of restoring our relationship with God on our own. That leads to the substitutionary atonement of Christ, which is discussed extensively throughout the Bible.

Church leaders throughout history have espoused various views of atonement. The debate over the "effects" or "atoning value" of Jesus's death has been long and drawn-out, going as far back as the Apostolic Fathers in the second century.

One reason is that the doctrine of atonement did not receive as much attention or face as much controversy as the trinitarian doctrine, the incarnation of Jesus, and the ramifications of Jesus literally and physically rising from the dead.

As such, Church fathers had less to say about atonement as other doctrines and their ideas were not thoroughly developed—leaving no actual creedal formula for the universal Church (see chart on the following page). But this doesn't mean atonement is a secondary doctrine that carries little weight in Christianity.

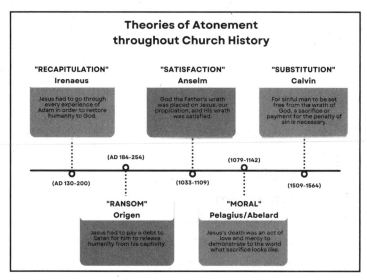

Theories of Atonement throughout Church History

"RECAPITULATION"
Irenaeus
Jesus had to go through every experience of Adam in order to restore humanity to God.

"SATISFACTION"
Anselm
God the Father's wrath was placed on Jesus, our propitiation, and His wrath was satisfied.

"SUBSTITUTION"
Calvin
For sinful man to be set free from the wrath of God, a sacrifice or payment for the penalty of sin is necessary.

(AD 184-254)   (1079-1142)
(AD 130-200)   (1033-1109)   (1509-1564)

"RANSOM"
Origen
Jesus had to pay a debt to Satan for him to release humanity from his captivity.

"MORAL"
Pelagius/Abelard
Jesus's death was an act of love and mercy to demonstrate to the world what sacrifice looks like.

Though not all "atonement theories" are biblically and theologically adequate explanations, "all of them . . . are illuminating and in some way widen our knowledge of this profound and crucial subject."[29]

The New Testament writers use several Greek terms to capture the nuance of what Christ did on the cross. Think of it like a jigsaw puzzle: piecing together the diverse meanings of "atonement" reveals a deeper and more elaborate picture of what Christ's substitution on the cross truly means for our salvation.

As you can see in the chart on the next page, atonement is a multi-faceted concept. In 1 Corinthians 15:3–5, Paul records an early creed that was probably in use within five years after Jesus's resurrection.

> For I delivered to you as of first importance what I also received: that Christ died for our sins in accordance with the Scriptures, that he was buried, that he was raised on the third day in accordance with the Scriptures, and that he appeared to Cephas, then to the twelve.

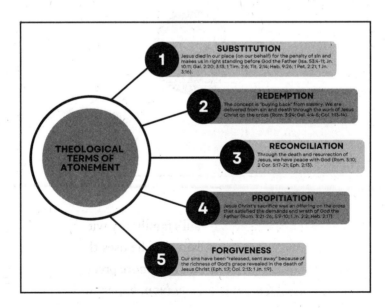

Paul uses two primary words for "atonement," "reconciliation," and "redemption." The first word is *apolytrōsis* "deliverance through substitution" (Romans 3:24; 8:23; 1 Corinthians 1:30; Ephesians 1:7, 14; 4:30; Colossians 1:14). It comes from two words, *apo*, "marker of dissociation or separation," and *lutroo*, "to redeem, to ransom."

The second word is *hilastērion*, "sacrifice or place of atonement." The English word is rendered *propitiation* (Romans 3:25; also used in Hebrews 9:5). John uses *hilasmos* in 1 John 2:2 ("He [Jesus] is the propitiation [*hilasmos*] for our sins") and *hilasmon* in 1 John 4:10 ("In this is love, not that we have loved God but that he loved us and sent his Son to be the propitiation [*hilasmon*] for our sins").

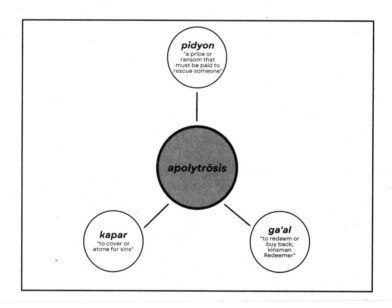

What is so interesting about Paul's familiarity with, and consistent application of, these Greek words is that he uses them to firmly tie Jesus's death to the Old Testament. To be more precise, *apolytrōsis* is derived from three Hebrew words: *pidyon*, *kapar*, and *ga'al*.

The original, technical meaning of *hilastērion* is not simply describing Jesus as an "atoning sacrifice." The imagery goes much deeper than that. The word comes from *kapporet*, by which Paul references the "Mercy Seat"—the space between the golden cherubim covering of the Ark of the Covenant that rests in the innermost sanctum of the Temple, the Holy of Holies.[30]

When expounding on the doctrine of atonement, Paul clearly pulls directly from the Old Testament, saying Christ's death is the fulfillment of the Levitical and sacrificial rituals.

Certainly, crucifixion was a horrific and barbaric way to die, but it by no means proves God to be a cruel heavenly Father—quite the opposite. Jesus's sacrificial death was an act of unconditional love which satisfied God's wrath toward sin and the works of the devil—not toward Jesus.[31]

We have all violated God's laws and are justly condemned to eternal separation from Him as a result. However, the Bible tells us that "God so loved the world that he gave his only Son" (John 3:16). As Dr. William Lane Craig puts it,

> By Christ's atoning death, God has made possible our pardon, so that we may escape condemnation and punishment. God legally imputed our sins to Christ, and he vicariously bore the just desert of those sins. Divine justice satisfied, God offers us the gift of His righteousness, that is to say, the imputation to us of that same property that He essentially exemplifies. Those who place their faith in Christ receive God's pardon and the imputation of a new legal status of righteousness in the place of condemnation.[32]

Starting with Jesus's death as fulfilled in the Jewish calendar and into the Pauline writings, the graphics paint a picture to help you grasp the doctrine of atonement.

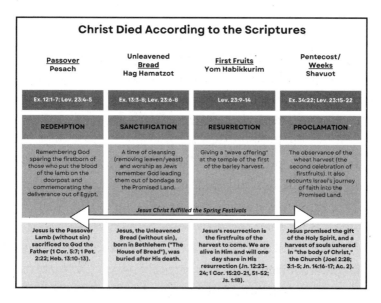

The doctrine of atonement reflects and combines the doctrines of God, man, sin, and the person of Jesus Christ magnificently, explaining both our need for salvation and the provision God made for us to receive it.[33]

Spiritual Results of Progressive Christianity

Robin Meyers, a fellow at the Westar Institute and the Jesus Seminar, teaches that Jesus did not come to save people from their sins but to liberate their minds from oppressive religion.[34]

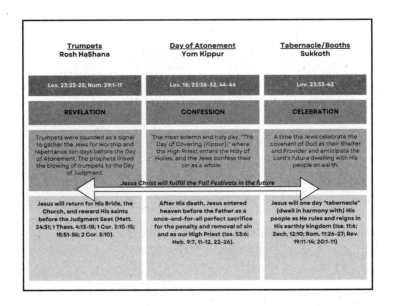

Trumpets Rosh HaShana	Day of Atonement Yom Kippur	Tabernacle/Booths Sukkoth
Lev. 23:23-25; Num. 29:1-11	Lev. 16; 23:26-32, 44-46	Lev. 23:33-43
REVELATION	**CONFESSION**	**CELEBRATION**
Trumpets were sounded as a signal to gather the Jews for worship and repentance ten days before the Day of Atonement. The prophets linked the blowing of trumpets to the Day of Judgment.	The most solemn and holy day, "The Day of Covering (Kippur)," where the High Priest enters the Holy of Holies, and the Jews confess their sin as a whole.	A time the Jews celebrate the covenant of God as their Shelter and Provider and anticipate the Lord's future dwelling with His people on earth.

Jesus Christ will fulfill the Fall Festivals in the future

Jesus will return for His Bride, the Church, and reward His saints before the Judgment Seat (Matt. 24:31; 1 Thess. 4:13-18; 1 Cor. 3:10-15; 15:51-58; 2 Cor. 5:10).	After His death, Jesus entered heaven before the Father as a once-and-for-all perfect sacrifice for the penalty and removal of sin and as our High Priest (Isa. 53:6; Heb. 9:7, 11-12, 22-26).	Jesus will one day "tabernacle" (dwell in harmony with) His people as He rules and reigns in His earthly kingdom (Isa. 11:6; Zech. 12:10; Rom. 11:26-27; Rev. 19:11-14; 20:1-11)

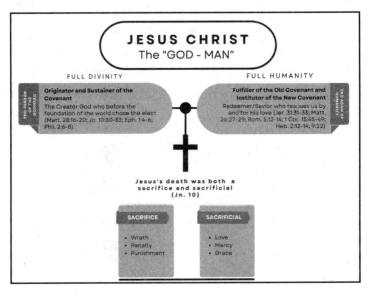

JESUS CHRIST
The "GOD - MAN"

FULL DIVINITY   FULL HUMANITY

2ND PERSON OF THE GODHEAD

Originator and Sustainer of the Covenant
The Creator God who before the foundation of the world chose the elect (Matt. 28:16-20; Jn. 10:30-33; Eph. 1:4-6; Phil. 2:6-8).

Fulfiller of the Old Covenant and Institutor of the New Covenant
Redeemer/Savior who rescues us by and for His love (Jer. 31:31-33; Matt. 26:27-29; Rom. 5:12-14; 1 Cor. 15:45-49; Heb. 2:12-14; 9:22)

2ND ADAM OF HUMANITY

Jesus's death was both a sacrifice and sacrificial (Jn. 10)

SACRIFICE
- Wrath
- Penalty
- Punishment

SACRIFICIAL
- Love
- Mercy
- Grace

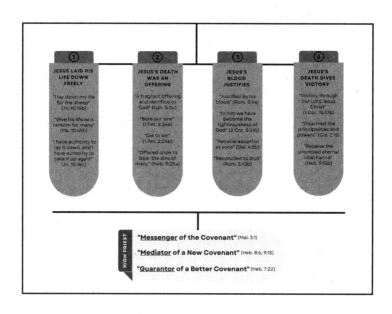

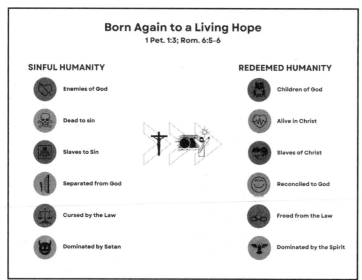

Other progressive Christians say the primary conclusion of atonement is that Jesus may be the "Savior" represented in Christianity, but that is not to say salvation cannot be found in other religions, too. Jesus is not the Lord and Savior of the world; He is simply a spiritual being who opened the door for humanity to draw closer to what Spong calls the "Ground of Being."[35]

Spiritual Results of Biblical Christianity

The atonement of Jesus is the greatest sacrifice in the history of the world, impacting the hearts, minds, and actions of people throughout history.

Jesus's death on the cross is about forgiveness. It is about God's grace for fallen man and His providential call to redeem humanity so that He can fellowship with us who are made in His own image once again.

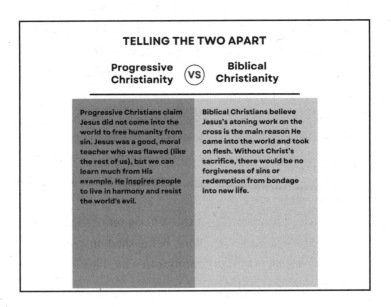

TELLING THE TWO APART

Progressive Christianity (VS) Biblical Christianity

Progressive Christians claim Jesus did not come into the world to free humanity from sin. Jesus was a good, moral teacher who was flawed (like the rest of us), but we can learn much from His example. He inspires people to live in harmony and resist the world's evil.

Biblical Christians believe Jesus's atoning work on the cross is the main reason He came into the world and took on flesh. Without Christ's sacrifice, there would be no forgiveness of sins or redemption from bondage into new life.

Exploring the depths of atonement shows us how much Jesus loves us. We can find confidence in knowing that salvation is bought and paid for by the infinite power and authority of Jesus Christ, and not by our own righteous acts.

Key Points to Use When Talking to Progressive Christians

Most progressive Christians view the substitutionary atonement of Jesus as an archaic and barbaric theology that crept into Christian doctrine. Here are four crucial points to remember when talking about Jesus's atonement.

- **Historical:** Jesus dying for the sins of humanity is the earliest and most indispensable doctrinal belief of Christianity.
- **Biblical:** Jesus's atonement is foreshadowed by God sacrificing an animal to cover Adam and Eve's nakedness in the Garden of Eden, was promised in the Davidic line, was announced by John the Baptist, was articulated in the Pauline epistles, and is memorialized in the tradition of communion.
- **Theological:** The meaning, effects, and outcomes of Jesus's atoning work on the cross can be understood by the multifaceted terms in the New Testament, such as "substitution," "redemption," "reconciliation," "propitiation," and "forgiveness."
- **Spiritual:** Atonement lies at the very center of the Bible's message. Without Jesus's blood being shed on the cross, there would be no atonement for our sins. There's absolutely no way around this.

CHAPTER 7

Hijacking Jesus's
Resurrection

I f Jesus did not rise from the dead, Christianity would be the biggest
scam religion in world history.

"Every sermon preached by every Christian in the New Testament centers on the resurrection," writes Peter Kreeft and Ronald
Tacelli in *Handbook of Christian Apologetics*. "The *gospel* or 'good
news' means essentially the news of Christ's resurrection. The message
that flashed across the ancient world, set hearts on fire, changed lives
and turned the world upside down was not 'love your neighbor.'"[1]

The iconic British theologian Michael Green aptly states

> Christianity does not hold the resurrection to be one
> among many tenets of belief. Without faith in the resur-
> rection *there would be no Christianity at all* [emphasis
> added]. The Christian church would never have begun; the
> Jesus-movement would have fizzled out like a damp squib
> with His execution. Christianity stands or falls with the

truth of the resurrection. Once disprove it, and you have disposed of Christianity.[2]

Historical Inquiries of Progressive Christianity

In delivering a lecture on his book *Saving Jesus from the Church* in Australia in 2016, Dr. Robin Meyers reasoned through the various problems with traditional Christianity and decried the too-many-to-count "abuses" of fundamentalism, gradually working his way into what he calls "three common myths" Christians subconsciously believe:

- The earliest Christians were orthodox.
- The Apostolic Fathers pushed back against heretics and false teaching.
- Roman politics had little or nothing to do with the formation of Christianity.

"According to First Corinthians 15, Paul did not believe in a physical resurrection," Meyers said. "Even though he wrote the earliest material in the New Testament, the supernatural accounts of Jesus were not added until either the eighth or ninth decade of the first century."[3]

Most progressive Christians believe that statement. They don't believe Jesus physically rose from the dead.

This is how Dr. Paula Fredriksen sees the development of the resurrection narrative:

With the crucifixion, Jesus' public ministry ends. When the evangelists resume their story, they recount the miracle to which they trace their own religious origins: Jesus' resurrection from the dead. Various individuals and communities in various situations—the disciples in Palestine, Paul and his Diaspora communities, the Christian writers of the second and third generations of the movement—responded in various ways to their belief in Jesus' resurrection. By analyzing their responses, we can begin to account for the development and diversity of the images of Jesus that we find in our New Testament texts. But an analysis of traditions originating in faith in the Risen Christ requires that we have in mind an image of their historical starting point, Jesus of Nazareth.[4]

Fredriksen is suggesting that after Jesus's shocking death, multiple disciples at different points in time concocted their own set of beliefs about Him and attempted to manufacture those beliefs as the version most accurately aligned with the facts. This, of course, split Christ-followers into various factions and even led James (Jesus's half-brother) and Paul to part ways.

Here are three main reasons progressive Christians don't believe in Jesus's resurrection:

- The earliest account of Jesus's resurrected appearances was written fifty years after the crucifixion, with limited details and incomplete facts.
- They believe early Christians copied from pagan resurrection stories to enshrine Jesus as a divine creature (most often citing *The World's Sixteen Crucified Saviors* by Kersey Graves as proof).
- Other "gospels" (by Peter, Thomas, Judas Iscariot, Philip, Mary, and others) about Jesus exclude details of, or contain no doctrinal beliefs regarding, His bodily resurrection.

Historical Inquiries of Biblical Christianity

The resurrection of Jesus is the most remarkable event in history. It played a central role in validating Jesus's divinity, confirming His message through eyewitnesses, and expanding the Gospel throughout the world.

Five primary historical attestations show that belief in a literal physical resurrection of Jesus Christ formed early.

The Gospels' Early and Detailed Narratives of the Resurrection

- **Mark's account is the earliest of the four gospels.** It was written well within the period of Jesus's contemporaries' living memory.[5] Good evidence suggests John Mark wrote a biographical account of Jesus from the Apostle Peter's firsthand testimony in the early 50s while staying in Rome[6] (Peter refers to Mark as his "son" in 1 Peter 5:13). Both Papias of Hierapolis (AD 60–130) and Irenaeus (AD 130–200) confirm the early writing to have come from John Mark.
- **Matthew's account is second.** Most biblical scholars agree that Matthew's gospel not only came shortly after Mark's (roughly AD 55–6), but that he used it as a reference when writing to Jewish Christians.
- **Luke's account is the third.** In his opening remarks, Luke mentions that "many have undertaken to compile a narrative" (1:1), pointing to the fact that he employed earlier documents to help compose his account of Jesus's life. Without hesitation, most New Testament scholars say those early gospels were written by Mark and Matthew. A realistic dating of Luke puts its publication

at AD 60 or before.[7] The Muratorian Canon (AD 190) states: "The third book of the gospel, that according to Luke, was compiled in his own name on Paul's authority by Luke the Physician, when after Christ's ascension Paul had taken him to be with him . . . yet neither did he see the Lord in the flesh."[8]

- **John's account is the fourth.** Most scholars place its composition before AD 90. However, most conservative scholars argue for a date between AD 64 and AD 70.[9] Although John's is not one of the "synoptic" gospels, and its structure is more Christological, it shares numerous "harmonies" with Matthew, Mark, and Luke.[10] Clement of Rome confirms the first-century date of John comes by citing it in his own work in AD 95–97.

An Early Traditional Creed
(1 Corinthians 15:3–7)

Dr. Gary Habermas, a leading New Testament scholar, dates specific historical facts found in 1 Corinthians by imagining a twenty-five-year timeline. Habermas marks Jesus's resurrection at AD 30, Paul's conversion around AD 33, and—based on Galatians 1:18—says Paul most likely "received" a creedal formula regarding Jesus's death and resurrection from two central figures in the early church, Peter and James, while visiting them in Jerusalem in AD 35.[11]

For I delivered to you as of first importance what I also received: that Christ died for our sins in accordance with the Scriptures, that he was buried, that he was raised on the third day in accordance with the Scriptures, and that he appeared to Cephas, then to the twelve. Then he appeared to more than five hundred brothers at one time, most of whom are still alive, though some have fallen asleep. Then he appeared to James, then to all the apostles. (1 Corinthians 15:3–7)

Habermas quotes the Jewish New Testament scholar Pinchas Lapide (1922–1997), who argued that the long, drawn-out sentence of 1 Corinthians 15:3–7 that is broken up by the "triple *hoti* clause"—"and that"—shows Paul was clearly passing on early church creedal tradition.[12]

Habermas's twenty-five-year timeline corroborates the idea of 1 Corinthians being written in AD 55, while Paul was wrapping up his third missionary journey (see Acts 18:23–20:14).

Another Early Traditional Creed
(1 Timothy 3:16)

Scholars estimate that Paul wrote 1 Timothy between AD 60 and 62, just a couple years before being martyred in Rome. That would mean the early creedal hymn about the incarnate Christ that Paul adds in 1 Timothy 3:16 was written before his letter to Timothy.[13]

1 Timothy 3:16 is fashioned in three couplets:

He was manifested in the flesh, vindicated by the Spirit,
seen by angels, proclaimed among the nations,
believed on in the world, taken up in glory.

This early creed features five profound truths the early Christians clearly believed:

1. Jesus took on flesh,
2. was empowered and raised from the dead by the Spirit,
3. was protected and vouched for by angels,

4. was proclaimed as the Savior of the world after His resurrection, and

5. ascended to Heaven (see Acts 1:1–11).[14]

The Apostles' Creed, AD 150s

The creed was an early second-century statement of the Christian faith embraced by both the Catholics and Protestants. The Apostles' Creed (even in the original and earlier form, "Old Roman Creed") affirms the belief in "the resurrection of the body (flesh)."

In explaining what the phrase "the resurrection of the body and the life everlasting" means, Alister McGrath writes, "In thinking of the resurrection of Christ, we are actually looking ahead to our own resurrection on the last day."[15]

Irenaeus's "Rule of Faith," AD 180

In *Against Heresies,* Irenaeus articulates doctrines that were well-established from the beginning of Christianity.

> The Church [believes] in one God, the Father Almighty, Maker of heaven and earth, and the sea, and all things that are them: and in one Christ Jesus, the Son of God, who became incarnate for our salvation . . . and [in] the resurrection from the dead, and ascension into heaven in the flesh of the beloved Christ Jesus, our Lord.[16] . . . Resurrecting the flesh is no problem for God. Since the Lord has power to infuse life into what He has fashioned, since the flesh is capable of being quickened, what remains to prevent its participation in in-corruption, which is a blissful and never-ending life granted by God.[17]

Here you have a second-century Church father confessing Jesus's physical resurrection in the earliest days of the Christian church.

Biblical Explanations of Progressive Christianity

Like his predecessors (Strauss, Bultmann, Schweitzer, and others mentioned previously), Marcus Borg rejects the historical accounts of Jesus's resurrection. In his classic book *Meeting Jesus Again for the First Time*, Borg provides several interpretations of Jesus's resurrection.

> In one sense, "Good Friday" and "Easter" are depictions of our "liberation from the powers." Powers that restrict us from communing with God and forces that pollute institutions and even bring about bondage in our lives.[18]

For Borg, the only way to interpret the "Good Friday" and "Easter" narratives is to see them as conjoined representations of a personal, transformative experience of a more pleasant and balanced faith in the spirit world, where one finds renewed hope and life.

Borg construes the story about Jesus raising Lazarus (John 11) this way:

> Just as the metaphor of blindness is found both in Jesus's teaching and in narratives about him, so is the metaphor of death. It is central to the story of the resurrection of Lazarus in John's gospel (11.1–44) . . . like many of the stories in John, it is symbolic, a purely metaphorical narrative.[19]

New York Times bestselling author Bart Ehrman sees Jesus raising the dead as an unusual ability to make people think they were healed. In the story of Jesus bringing a young girl back to life (Mark 5:21–43), Ehrman says He "resuscitated" her; He didn't bring her back from the dead. The story, he says, was a "theatrical" means to make it seem as though Jesus is the "resurrection and the life" (John 11:25).[20]

Building on eighteenth-century liberal scholar Hermann Samuel Reimarus's thoughts, Ehrman writes in *Jesus Before the Gospels* that most people in the first century were illiterate. They couldn't write things down but relied on their faulty memories. This created many conflicting recollections that eventually drove them to write down details about Jesus they didn't know to be accurate, including the "resurrection" story.[21]

Most progressive scholars regard Diarmaid MacCulloch as having produced some of the most definitive work on Christianity. In *Christianity: The First Three Thousand Years*, he writes,

> Nowhere in the New Testament is there a description of the Resurrection: it was beyond the capacity or the intention of the writers to describe it, and all they described were its effects. The New Testament is thus a literature with a blank at its centre; yet this blank is also its intense focus.[22]

Biblical Explanations of Biblical Christianity

Throughout the pages of the New Testament, the writers underscore the importance of Jesus's physical resurrection:

- It confirms Jesus's teachings were divinely inspired (John 5:1–46; 6:60–71).
- It validates Him as the Son of God (Acts 2:22–36).
- It guarantees our salvation (Hebrews 7:23–25).

- It promises we will also have glorious bodies in the future (1 Corinthians 15:42–44; Philippians 3:20–21).
- It proves the Second Coming of Jesus will take place in the future (Revelation 19:11–21).
- It testifies that we will reign with Christ in our glorious bodies someday (John 6:50; 1 Corinthians 15:22; 2 Corinthians 5:1–5; Colossians 3:1–4).

The New Testament writers also affirm that Jesus was raised from the dead and has taken His eternal position at the right hand of the Father:

- Jesus defeated sin and death (Acts 2:24).
- Christ is seated at the right hand of the Father in the heavenly places (Ephesians 1:20).
- Jesus is the Author of Life raised from the dead (Acts 3:15).
- Jesus triumphed over every power and authority (Colossians 2:13–15).
- Jesus is called "the firstborn of the dead" (Colossians 1:18; Revelation 1:5).

The canonical gospels make several references to Jesus's physical and post-resurrection bodies.

- Jesus implied His resurrected body would be the one He occupied in life: "Destroy this temple [body], and in three days I will raise it [the same body] up" (John 2:19).

John adds, "But he was speaking about the temple of his body" (2:21).

- Speaking of the body that was crucified, Jesus told His disciples, "See my hands and my feet, that it is I myself! Touch me, and see. For a spirit does not have flesh and bones as you see I have" (Luke 24:39). This proves His resurrected body was physical.
- Jesus ate on several occasions (Luke 24:41–43; Acts 10:41).
- Jesus proved He had risen in the same physical body by showing His crucifixion scars on two occasions (Luke 24:40; John 20:27). Had His resurrected body been only a spiritual or metaphysical manifestation, some physical evidence of the body He occupied in life would have been left behind.[23]

John the Apostle Speaks of Interacting with Jesus's Physical Resurrected Body

John, writing sometime after AD 85, recounts extraordinary physical interactions with the resurrected Christ, including:

That which was from the beginning, which *we have heard*, which *we have seen with our eyes*, which *we looked upon* and *have touched with our hands*, concerning the word of life . . . (1 John 1:1; emphasis added)

In responding to the heretical teaching of his day that Jesus didn't come in the flesh, the Apostle John writes, "By this you know the Spirit of God: every spirit that confesses that Jesus Christ has come in the flesh is from God" (1 John 4:2).

Dr. Norman Geisler and I were conducting a Q&A session with a group of pastors who asked us to give some context to that passage. Geisler explained that "has come" uses the perfect participle in Greek (*elēlythota*, "to come to; to go; to return")— implying that Christ came in the flesh and still remains in the flesh (after resurrection). I then pointed out that John used the same term for "flesh" (Greek *sarx*) again in 2 John 7, "those who do not confess the coming of Jesus Christ in the *flesh* [emphasis added]," directly confirming that John believed Jesus's resurrection was literal and physical.

Paul Corroborates Jesus's Physical Resurrected Body

Paul went from being a pharisaical zealot who murdered Christians to becoming the most recognizable follower of Jesus Christ. He later was martyred by the Romans for his faith (see Acts 9:1–9; 22:6–11; 26:12–19).

If Paul didn't believe Jesus rose physically from the dead, he never would have declared that the same mortal bodies we possess on Earth will take on immortality for all eternity. Yet he did so repeatedly (see Romans 6:12; 8:11; 1 Corinthians 15:53; 2 Corinthians 4:10; Colossians 1:22).

Paul argued that Jesus was Savior and Judge based on the indisputable proof of His physical resurrection (see Acts 17:31; 1 Corinthians 15:1–11). Later in his epistles, Paul speaks of Jesus's resurrection as giving "life to your mortal bodies" (Romans 8:11).

Thus, it is well established in the annals of the New Testament that Jesus's post-resurrection appearances were in a physical, Spirit-dominated body. Seventeen New Testament passages confirm that Jesus was seen in His resurrected body.

FIRST APPEARANCE: to Mary Magdalene as she remained at the tomb (John 20:11–17).	SECOND APPEARANCE: to the other women who were also returning to the tomb (Matthew 28:9–10).	THIRD APPEARANCE: to Peter (Luke 24:34; 1 Corinthians 15:5).
FOURTH APPEARANCE: to the disciples as they walked on the road to Emmaus (Mark 16:12–13; Luke 24:13–31).	FIFTH APPEARANCE: to the ten disciples (Mark 16:14; Luke 24:36–51; John 20:19–23).	SIXTH APPEARANCE: to the eleven disciples a week after His resurrection (John 20:26–29).
SEVENTH APPEARANCE: to seven disciples by the Sea of Galilee (John 21:1–23).	EIGHTH APPEARANCE: to five hundred others (1 Corinthians 15:6).	NINTH APPEARANCE: to James, Jesus's brother (1 Corinthians 15:7).
TENTH APPEARANCE: to the eleven disciples on the mountain in Galilee (Matthew 28:16–20).	ELEVENTH APPEARANCE: at the time of the ascension (Luke 24:44–53; Acts 1:3–9).	TWELFTH APPEARANCE: to Stephen just before his martyrdom (Acts 7:55–56).
THIRTEENTH APPEARANCE: to Paul on the road to Damascus (Acts 9:3–6; 22:6–11; 26:13–18).	FOURTEENTH APPEARANCE: to Paul in Arabia (Galatians 1:12–17).	FIFTEENTH APPEARANCE: to Paul in the temple (Acts 9:26–27; 22:17–21).
SIXTEENTH APPEARANCE: to Paul while he was in prison in Caesarea (Acts 23:11).	SEVENTEENTH APPEARANCE: to the Apostle John (Revelation 1:12–20).[24]	

Theological Arguments of Progressive Christianity

The website of Bethel Congregational United Church of Christ in the Portland area reads, "Progressive Christian Beliefs Are Rooted in Jesus." If someone is not distinctly familiar with progressive Christianity and not well-versed in biblical Christianity, they could easily buy into the deceptive phraseology of the statement below:

> We believe that God's will and way were revealed in Jesus of Nazareth. We believe that the historical Jesus, the Jewish Rabbi carpenter who lived in ancient Palestine, became the Christ as his followers encountered him in their midst after his earthly death. The Holy Spirit awakened them to the power of Jesus' presence in their midst. Jesus came alive when they trusted that his love, guidance, support, comfort and challenge remained with them even though his physical body did not. Jesus' life, death and resurrection provide the inspiration and challenge for us to live as followers of Jesus today.[25]

A casual reading of this progressive belief statement may sound like it affirms the literal physical resurrection of Jesus Christ. But it doesn't.

Here's how we can tell:

It insinuates that Jesus "came alive," not by the Spirit who raised Him from the dead, but through His followers. Jesus "lives on" through the Church as it advances His moral and charitable teachings. It does not infer a literal bodily resurrection.

The belief statement also casually announces that Jesus's "physical body did not" remain with the disciples after the crucifixion. Another spiritual overtone that denies a literal-bodily resurrection.

Given what you have learned so far about Richard Rohr, you may be surprised to learn he says he believes Jesus *physically* rose from the dead.[26]

But then he clarifies that by writing, "If matter is inhabited by God, then matter is somehow eternal."[27]

Rohr is arguing from a panentheistic worldview that teaches there is no separation between the natural realm (matter) and the supernatural. When he says he believes Jesus physically rose, he is implying that Jesus is one with creation, as we all are; Jesus's death and resurrection are the results of a continuing process of self-emptying through ongoing incarnations.

R. C. Symes shares this view.

In his essay, "The Resurrection Myths about Jesus: A Progressive Christian Interpretation," Symes suggests that, according to Paul,

> Christ's resurrected body was not a resuscitated physical body, but a new body of a spiritual/celestial nature . . . Paul never says that the earthly body becomes immortal. Jesus' earthly body rotted in the grave.[28]

Theological Arguments of Biblical Christianity

Trying to make sense of what Jesus's post-resurrection body became is not easy.

The first thing we must understand is that Jesus rose physically in the same body that was buried in the tomb. Dr. Robert Gundry, in his excellent work *Soma in Biblical Theology*, notes that the Greek word *sōma*, when describing a human person, always refers to a physical body. So when speaking of how Paul discusses Jesus's resurrected body in 1 Corinthians 15, Gundry notes,

> [T]he consistent and exclusive use of *sōma* for the physical body in anthropological contexts resists dematerialization of the resurrection, whether by idealism or by existentialism.[29]

This is extremely important, because "Paul uses *sōma* precisely because the physicality of the resurrection is central to his soteriology."[30]

However, as Ryrie points out, Jesus's body was also different because it wasn't subject to normal physical limitations.

> For instance, after the resurrection He could pass through closed doors (Jn 20:19), but most important He cannot die ever again (Ro 6:9).[31]

Although Jesus's post-resurrection body is physical, it is also spiritual. The Greek words used to describe it are *sōma pneumatikos*, which means "immortal and imperishable." The term indicates "nonphysical," not "immaterial." At no time did Jesus's natural body become an immaterial body.

Essentially, His resurrected body is a physical, Spirit-dominated body. As Ryrie puts it,

> His was not a resurrection of "influence" or "spirit." The resurrection does not mean simply that His memory lives on, but it was a physical, bodily resurrection. Those bodily characteristics of His resurrection body were felt and seen by the disciples (Lk 24:39; Jn 20:27), and He demonstrated certain physical functions when He ate with them (Lk 24:42–43).[32]

Take, for instance, the two disciples who didn't recognize Jesus when He encountered them on the road to Emmaus. This does not mean

Jesus appeared as a "spirit" or "immaterial" manifestation. Notice what Luke 24:16 says: "their eyes were kept from recognizing him."

Considering the gravity of the circumstance, Wayne Grudem supplies a few fair points:

> Jesus did not look exactly as he did before he died, for in addition to the initial amazement of the disciples at what they apparently thought could not happen, there was probably sufficient difference in his physical appearance for Jesus not to be immediately recognized. Perhaps that difference in appearance was simply the difference between a man who lived a life of suffering, hardship, and grief, and whose body was restored to its full youthful appearance of perfect health: Though Jesus' body was still a physical body, it was raised as a transformed body, never able again to suffer, be weak or ill, or die; it had "put on immortality" (1 Cor. 15:53).[33]

Grudem further observes that Jesus's physical body points to God's original order of material creation being absolutely good. The fact that Jesus's body was resurrected gives us hope that we will one day receive our resurrected bodies as well and live forever with Him in the "new heavens and a new earth in which righteousness dwells" (2 Peter 3:13).[34]

Through the redemption of Jesus, creation will experience a reversal of material decay to material renewal. Things will one day be restored to their original state, as God intended from the beginning (Romans 8:21).

Spiritual Results of Progressive Christianity

A progressive writer claims the term "body of Christ" Paul uses in Romans 12:5 and 1 Corinthians 12:27 means Jesus's followers carried forth His message and, therefore, represent His "body" and seek to live out His legacy as they overcome bad tendencies with good.

> When Christians talk about the resurrection of Christ, they may be proclaiming that death did not have the last word in the Jesus story because his followers were raised up to be his new body. When they say that they believe in the resurrection of the dead, they may be proclaiming that no matter how much a person has given in to destructive tendencies, new life is always possible.[35]

The "faith" of progressive Christians does not rely on the physical resurrection of Jesus Christ, who conquered sin and death. To them, "resurrection" is a mystical revelation symbolizing the individual's spiritual journey of finding renewal and peace with whatever their version of God might be. Or, as many progressive Christians are prone to say, "The Christian faith is a journey, not a destination."

Resurrection, to them, is about the Spirit reviving the hearts of those who seek to be transformed by "rebirth," which is the cosmic pattern that reverberates in all things.

Spiritual Results of Biblical Christianity

Erwin Lutzer has the best description of the meaning and power of Jesus's resurrection.

> The fact of Christ's resurrection gives us hope as we face death, not because we are blind to death's horrors, but because we look with confidence upon Jesus of Nazareth. The resurrection is the Great Reversal, the one reality

which gives us the assurance that no other realities of our existence need ever permanently discourage us.[36]

That is so true.

And so, we wait with great anticipation for Christ to return. Then He will transform our sinful bodies to be like His glorified body (Philippians 3:20–21).

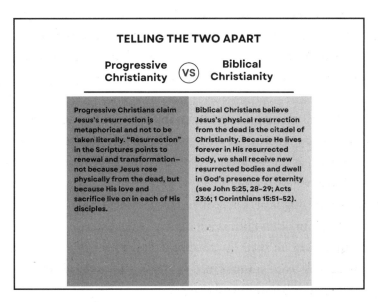

TELLING THE TWO APART

Progressive Christianity	vs	Biblical Christianity
Progressive Christians claim Jesus's resurrection is metaphorical and not to be taken literally. "Resurrection" in the Scriptures points to renewal and transformation— not because Jesus rose physically from the dead, but because His love and sacrifice live on in each of His disciples.		Biblical Christians believe Jesus's physical resurrection from the dead is the citadel of Christianity. Because He lives forever in His resurrected body, we shall receive new resurrected bodies and dwell in God's presence for eternity (see John 5:25, 28–29; Acts 23:6; 1 Corinthians 15:51–52).

Key Points to Use When Talking to Progressive Christians

Be mindful of the fact that progressive Christianity repudiates a literal physical resurrection for a more sumptuous view of "resuscitation," while some progressive Christians employ metaphors and motifs to reinterpret the Easter story. Refute those arguments by remembering:

- **Historical:** Multiple eyewitnesses attested to Jesus's physical resurrection, including credible firsthand testimonies from Peter (written down by John Mark), Matthew, Luke, and Paul—who passed along early creeds affirming Jesus's death, burial, and physical resurrection.

- **Biblical:** The canonical gospel writers discuss multiple post-mortem encounters with Jesus and attest to the fact that His physical resurrection validated His claims to be the Son of God (see Acts 2:22–36).
- **Theological:** Jesus's resurrected body is the same physical body that was crucified. Jesus's resurrected body was not "immaterial," but "spiritual" (Greek, *sōma pneumatikos*, meaning "immortal and imperishable").
- **Spiritual:** Christians who believe in a physical resurrection of Jesus Christ are waiting for His return and anticipating the transformation of our sinful bodies into resurrected bodies free from the power of sin and death.

CHAPTER 8

Hijacking Jesus's

Second Coming

et's circle back to Dr. Robin Meyers's lecture in Australia. At the
end, he says rather humorously, "Perhaps you're waiting for the
Second Coming. You think the Second Coming is really, really important. Could that be because deep down you were really disappointed
in the first one?"[1]

Progressive Christians often suggest biblical Christians are
somehow disappointed in Jesus's first coming, so they concocted a
doctrine that says He will return and rule the earth with an iron fist.
Or they refer to fundamentalist "fearmongering" and sensational
imagery of doomsday theology to illustrate how ludicrous End Times
prophecy is.[2] Bradley Jersak writes,

> I've heard the returning Christ depicted as *Braveheart*'s
> William Wallace—face smudged blue with war paint, mus-
> cles rippling, claymore flashing, on a righteous rampage.
> Perhaps you have never heard Christ's glorious victory

reduced to a blood-soaked military campaign, in which Jesus personally kills millions of people, his white robes soaked in their blood—literally.[3]

Why do progressive Christians so adamantly oppose the doctrine of the Second Coming of Jesus?

Historical Inquiries of Progressive Christianity

There is much internal debate among progressive Christians about the apocalyptic imagery Jesus discussed in the gospels and the origin and meaning of the eschatological prophecies.

However, historically speaking, they most commonly interpret them as a "nonliteral" or "spiritualized" understanding of Jesus's teachings about His return.

Princeton Theological Seminary's Dale Allison breaks down the assorted apocalyptic views amongst many of the prominent liberal scholars in the past three hundred years[4]—many of whom, it must be said, are nonreligious:

- **Reimarus:** "Jesus envisioned an earthly kingdom in Jerusalem, with himself on the throne, a kingdom that would rout the Romans and make real the paradisical oracles of the Old Testament. Because none of this transpired, the disciples invented the second coming."[5]
- **David F. Strauss:** "If Jesus sincerely foretold his own second coming on the clouds of heaven, then we must dismiss him as a fanatic."[6]
- **Tom Wright:** "Passionately promotes a Jesus who used eschatological metaphors to prophesy what in fact came to pass in the first century—his own resurrection, the

ecclesia, Jerusalem's violent demise. When Jesus spoke of the Son of Man coming on the clouds of heaven, he was not fantasizing about a sky ride on condensed vapors but was being poetic. He meant that the clouds of judgment were gathering."[7]

Whether it stems from liberals teaching that Jesus failed to overthrow the Roman empire and establish His Kingdom or that the disciples naively thought Jesus would return in their lifetime, the bottom line is progressive Christians believe the Second Coming has nothing to do with Jesus returning physically to Earth in the near future.

Historical Inquiries of Biblical Christianity

The canonical gospels record Jesus mentioning His visible, physical return to Earth on multiple occasions: Matthew 16:27; 24:27, 30–31, 44; Luke 12:40; 21:27–28; John 14:3; and Revelation 22:12.

Paul wrote two key passages discussing the literal return of Jesus in detail. The first, 1 Thessalonians 4:13–5:11, was written in AD 50 or 51 when Paul was in Corinth (see Acts 18:12–17). The second, 1 Corinthians 15, was written as he was wrapping up his third missionary journey, around AD 55 (see Acts 18:23–20:14).

In both passages, Paul describes the physical event of Christ's return and the effects it will have on our physical bodies, transforming them from "mortality" to "immortality" (see 1 Thessalonians 4:16; 1 Corinthians 15:53).

Shortly after the last of the apostles died in the late first century, *The Epistle of Barnabas* was published. The fifteenth chapter discusses the millennium reign of Jesus Christ, stating that "everything shall come to an end" and "when His Son shall come" He will abolish the Antichrist, judge the ungodly, and bring restoration to the earth.[8]

The early church historian Eusebius cites the Greek apostolic father Papias as believing in a literal return of Jesus to Earth: "there will be a millennium after the resurrection from the dead, when the personal reign of Christ will be established on this earth."[9]

In *Against Heresies*, Irenaeus elaborates on what will happen when Jesus Christ returns physically to Earth: (1) "the righteous receiving the promise of the inheritance," (2) "creation itself, being restored," (3) "renew the inheritance of the earth," (4) "new flesh which rises again," (5) "righteous shall bear rule upon their rising from the dead," and (6) "animals . . . become peaceful and harmonious among each other."[10]

These are just a few examples that show the teachings about Jesus returning to Earth came early and abundantly.[11]

Biblical Explanations of Progressive Christianity

Adolf von Harnack (1851–1930) paved the way for a classic liberal interpretation of eschatology. He believed that the real message behind Jesus's apocalyptic teachings had nothing to do with a future earthly reign, but to promote the "ethic of love."[12]

Another figure who spent a lot of time debunking "prophetic literalism" was none other than Nobel Peace Prize winner Albert Schweitzer (1875–1965). In his two most recognizable works, *The Mystery of the Kingdom of God* (1906) and *The Quest of the Historical Jesus* (1910), he characterizes Jesus as a "credulous" spiritual leader who foolishly believed He and His followers would defeat the Jews' Roman oppressors. But He was arrested and crucified, ending any hope of Him reigning on Earth.

Christopher Hays, a leading voice among progressives on the return of Jesus, served as editor for the book *When the Son of Man Didn't Come: A Constructive Proposal on the Delay of the Parousia.* In an essay called "Was Jesus Wrong about the End?" Hays states rather pointedly that "Jesus definitely prophesied that he would be back before the end of the first century. And since we are still here, it seems like he was pretty wrong!"[13]

Hays bases this on several statements Jesus made in the gospels:

> "Truly, I say to you, there are some standing here who will not taste death until they see the kingdom of God after it has come with power." (Mark 9:1)
> "Truly, I say to you, this generation will not pass away until all these things take place." (Mark 13:30)
> "Be on guard, keep awake. For you do not know when the time will come." (Mark 13:33)
> "You will not have gone through all the towns of Israel before the Son of Man comes." (Matthew 10:23)

According to Marcus Borg, Jesus was not transfixed by end-time prophecy.

> It was one of the things he believed, but not the central conviction driving his mission. It would mean that Jesus was passionate about his message, and also believed that God might very well act decisively in the near future.[14]

John Dominic Crossan, a highly regarded progressive scholar, argues that the best way to understand the apocalyptic Kingdom Jesus mentioned is to see it as Wisdom personified, not some future King who will come with fiery judgment to destroy the earth.[15]

Robin Meyers insinuates that the early church used the apocalyptic writings about Jesus's Second Coming to minimize evil in the world and cover for Jesus's incorrect predictions about the future.[16]

In his book *Jesus Unexpected: Ending the End Times to Become the Second Coming*, Keith Giles writes that the only way to understand Jesus's apocalyptic teachings is to frame them in the first century.

> If you understand that Jesus is talking only about the coming destruction of Jerusalem and the Temple, and if you understand how to read Apocalyptic Hyperbole correctly, then you've got no problem at all. . . . [E]verything Jesus describes in the Olivet Discourse actually did transpire within forty years of his prophecy, so there were some standing there listening to him who were absolutely alive to see every single thing he predicted come to pass in absolute fulfillment of his prediction.[17]

Progressive Christians think much of what Jesus taught about the "end times" had to do with either His insurrection or the future destruction of Jerusalem in AD 70. Anything beyond that, they say, is nothing but fairy tale talk.

Biblical Explanations of Biblical Christianity

Perhaps the single most crucial example of Jesus talking about His Second Coming is found in the Olivet Discourse—but this passage is often misunderstood.

For example, was Jesus simply detailing the future destruction of the Temple in AD 70, or was He talking about returning to the earth as King?

Let's look at three passages to find out.

The Olivet Discourse.
(Matthew 24–25; Mark 13; Luke 21)

Jesus left the temple and was going away, when his disciples came to point out to him the buildings of the temple. [Luke 21:5] And while some were speaking of the temple, how it was adorned with noble stones and offerings [Mark 13:1b] one of his disciples said to him, "Look, Teacher, what wonderful stones and what wonderful buildings!" (Matthew 24:1)

Here we read that while Jesus was leaving the Temple near the Mount of Olives (on the east side of Jerusalem, overlooking the Temple), a disciple drew His attention to the magnificent structure (built by Herod for the Jews; 20 BC–AD 64).[18]

Jesus responded,

As for these things that you see, the days will come when there will not be left here one stone upon another that will not be thrown down. (Luke 21:6)

Notice, Jesus's response has to do with the physical destruction of the Temple because that is the context in which it was raised. (Jesus will later provide more details of Jerusalem's destruction in Luke 21:20–24).

It's not surprising that the disciples were startled by Jesus's response, which triggered them to ask more probing questions.

And as he sat on the Mount of Olives opposite the temple, Peter and James and John and Andrew asked him privately, "Tell us, when will these things be, and what will be the sign when all these things are about to be accomplished

[Mark 13:3–4; Luke 21:7] and what will be the sign of your coming and of the end of the age?" (Matthew 24:3)

The four disciples ask Jesus three pertinent questions:

1. When will these things happen?
2. What will be the sign or signs of your coming?
3. When will be the end of the age?

Bible teacher Thomas Ice writes,

> The disciples were probably thinking that if Jesus had just announced the destruction of the Temple, it must mean that the end of the age was at hand and that it was the time for Him to be revealed in Jerusalem as the messianic King. If these events were indeed imminent, then they wanted to know when they would occur and how Jesus' messianic appearance would be announced to the Jewish nation.[19]

The disciples naturally interpreted Jesus's power over sin and death to mean the coming restoration was about to happen (see Ezekiel 36:36–37; Joel 2:28–29; Zechariah 12:10). Therefore, it is fitting that their first question is about the Temple's destruction.

Jesus answers in Luke 21:20–24.

> "But when you see Jerusalem surrounded by armies, then know that its desolation has come near. Then let those who are in Judea flee to the mountains, and let those who are inside the city depart, and let not those who are out in the country enter it, for these are days of vengeance, to fulfill all that is written. Alas for women who are pregnant and for those who are nursing infants in those days!

For there will be great distress upon the earth and wrath against this people. They will fall by the edge of the sword and be led captive among all nations, and Jerusalem will be trampled underfoot by the Gentiles, until the times of the Gentiles are fulfilled."

Jesus gives a chilling portrayal of Jerusalem's destruction in AD 70, when Israel will be "surrounded" or under siege by her enemies.[20] He then proceeds, in Matthew 24:4–28, to answer the next two questions by giving a broad overview of the catastrophic events that will unfold during the Tribulation period, which are kicked off by what He calls the "beginning of sorrows" or "birth pains." The account in Matthew runs parallel to what John wrote in Revelation.

Matthew 24:4–7 First Half of the Tribulation	Revelation 6:1–14 First Half of the Tribulation
False teaching (v. 4–5)	The Antichrist and false teaching (v. 1–2)
Wars and rumors of wars (v. 6)	Bloody war (v. 3–4)
Famines (v. 7)	Famines (v. 5–6)
Earthquakes (v. 7)	Earthquakes (v. 12–14)

Jesus concludes by telling the disciples,

"Immediately after the tribulation of those days the sun will be darkened, and the moon will not give its light, and the stars will fall from heaven, and the powers of the heavens will be shaken." (Matthew 24:29)

Jesus's use of the word "immediately" directly links His return to the "great distress" of Tribulation laid out in Matthew 24:15–28.

In *The NIV Application Commentary*, Michael Wilkins explains the context of Matthew 24:29:

> Jesus uses typical apocalyptic imagery as he alludes here to passages such as Isaiah 13:10 and 34:4 to describe his coming with a mixture of literal and figurative language. God will cause the skies to be darkened and the heavenly bodies to be disturbed. Such language may point to both physical phenomena and political and spiritual disruptions. The darkness at Jesus' crucifixion was an indication that he had conquered the forces of evil on the cross, and the darkness during his second coming is an indication that he will now exert his rule over all forces, especially those of the demonic prince of the powers of the air.[21]

Jesus then addresses the third and final question about His return to Earth (see Matthew 24:30–36; 25:31–33; Mark 13:24–27; Luke 21:25–28).

> "Then will appear in heaven the sign of the Son of Man, and then all the tribes of the earth will mourn, and they will see the Son of Man coming on the clouds of heaven with power and great glory." (Matthew 24:30, see also Mark 13:26; Luke 21:27)

Jesus paints a picture of His triumphal return, when He will rescue His people from their enemies and Israel will recognize their Messiah (see Zechariah 12:9–14). The word "sign" in Greek can mean "banner," and the reference to "clouds of heaven" alludes to Daniel 7:13.

Jesus then makes three statements that progressive Christians misconstrue. The first statement is found in Matthew 24:34,

> "Truly, I say to you, this generation will not pass away until all these things take place."

Many progressive Christians wrongly assume the "generation" Jesus was talking about were the people who would live to see the Temple's destruction. However, that is simply an improper way of interpreting the Olivet Discourse. In context, Jesus has just spoken about the Tribulation. Therefore, it is safe to conclude that Jesus was referring to the generation of people living through the Tribulation, those waiting for his return (future believers) must recognize that their redemption is drawing near (Luke 21:28).

The second statement is found in Matthew 24:36,

> "But concerning that day and hour no one knows, not even the angels of heaven, nor the Son, but the Father only."

Progressive Christians claim Jesus openly admits He doesn't know anything about the future, thereby acknowledging He isn't God. However, that is just an erroneous interpretation. Jesus was speaking from His vantage point as a human—not as the Son of God. (See the discussion on Jesus's two natures in chapter 3).

The final statement is recorded in Matthew 25:31–33:

> "When the Son of Man comes in his glory, and all the angels with him, then he will sit on his glorious throne. Before him will be gathered all the nations, and he will separate people one from another as a shepherd separates

the sheep from the goats. And he will place the sheep on his right, but the goats on the left."

Progressive Christians believe this passage is Jesus foretelling the judgment that will be placed on those who suppressed His social charity and neglected to care for the outcast and the oppressed—not something to do with the judgment of all mankind for whether they accepted His gift of salvation in life.

In *The Coming of the Son of Man: New Testament Eschatology for an Emerging Church*, Andrew Perriman introduces the passage as imagery that speaks to the rulers of Jesus's day.

> If you're wondering about the sheep and goats judgment when the Son of Man would come in his glory to judge the nations (Matt. 25:31–46), this was not a comprehensive final judgment. It was a limited judgment of the peoples of the Greek-Roman world, within a limited timeframe, according to how they had responded to the presence of Jesus' suffering emissaries.[22]

However, the proper interpretation of Matthew 25:31–46 is that it speaks of a future judgment whereby Jesus will return and separate those who obeyed Him (sheep) and those who rejected Him (goats). In Matthew 25:31–46, Jesus reaches the climax of the Olivet Discourse with a scene detailing His coming judgment on the Gentiles who survive the Tribulation. The "goats" (unbelievers) are sent to Hell, and the "sheep" (believers) are allowed to enter the Millennial Kingdom.[23]

This rendering of the passage makes sense in the context of Jesus's parabolic teachings of the virgins with the lamps (25:1–13) and the servants who invested or buried the talents (25:14–30). It also fits the prophetic timetable Jesus introduced to the disciples.

The Ascension of Jesus

And when he had said these things, as they were looking on,
he was lifted up, and a cloud took him out of their sight. And
while they were gazing into heaven as he went, behold, two
men stood by them in white robes, and said, "Men of Galilee, why do you stand looking into heaven? This Jesus, who
was taken up from you into heaven, will come in the same
way as you saw him go into heaven." (Acts 1:9–11)

Soon after Jesus was enveloped by the clouds, the disciples received
a message from two angels about His return. It is hard to deny what
Luke meant when he said in Greek, "in the same way or manner"
(*houtōs hos tropos*). He is literally saying, "Jesus will descend from
Heaven in the same way that He went up." The language shows Jesus's
return to be personal, physical, and glorious.

Furthermore, most scholars believe the two angels were refer-
encing Zechariah 14:4, which prophesied that the Messiah, Jesus
Christ, would return and "stand on the Mount of Olives," giving
additional physical descriptions of Jesus's return to Earth.

The Day of the Lord

For you yourselves are fully aware that the day of the Lord
will come like a thief in the night. (1 Thessalonians 5:2)

The term "Day of the Lord" refers to Jesus appearing to vindicate
His people and bring judgment on the wicked (*parousia*; mentioned in
1 Thessalonians 2:19; 3:13; 4:15). This is separate from the Rapture (see
1 Thessalonians 4:13–18). Yet Paul places the Rapture and the "Day of
the Lord" together: the "Day of the Lord" includes multifarious

activities, such as the Rapture, the Great Tribulation period, and the establishment of the Millennial Kingdom.

When you look closely at the "Day of the Lord," you will discover that every description prophesied by a messenger of God is about a literal activity that will happen sometime in the future:

- God carrying out the Great Tribulation period on Earth (Matthew 24:4–18; Revelation 4:1–19:21)
- God judging His enemies (Isaiah 2:12)
- God pouring out His wrath on unbelievers (Isaiah 3:16–24; Jeremiah 30:7; Zephaniah 1:14–18)
- God saving His people from His wrath (1 Thessalonians 5:9)

The apostles undeniably believed Jesus fulfilled the Scriptures literally in the flesh and, therefore, preached and taught that He would return in physical form to rule over the earth.[24]

Theological Arguments of Progressive Christianity

As one would imagine, progressives put forth a host of theological arguments concerning the Second Coming. The more mystical ones, such as Richard Rohr, believe it is not a future one-time event when Jesus returns to Earth with fire and brimstone, but is the continual rebirthing of creation that grows brighter and brighter as the material world takes on more of the oneness of God.

Incarnation did not just happen two thousand years ago. It has been working throughout the entire arc of time, and will continue. This is expressed in the common phrase the "Second Coming of Christ," which was unfortunately read as a threat ("Wait till your dad gets home!"), whereas it should more accurately be spoken of as the "Forever Coming of Christ," which is anything but a threat. In fact, it is the ongoing promise of eternal resurrection.[25]

David Felten and Jeff Procter-Murphy see the language of destruction and persecution in Jesus's apocalyptic teachings as metaphors for Roman oppression.

As Christians entered the story, they took over that phrasing of expectancy and aimed it squarely at the oppressive rule of Rome. While the New Testament is aglow with "Christ is coming!" the notion of the second coming was, for the early Christian, a very specific way of expressing hope in overcoming their suffering under the heel of empire. It was essentially resistance literature hiding the promise of triumph in fantastical images and language. The "end," as announced in Revelation, is not the end of the world, but the end of the Roman Empire. (Take heed, present-day imperial powers!)[26]

They deny a literal second coming of Jesus and interpret the earth-dwelling Church as the "second coming" that is called to bring hope to a world filled with fear.[27]

Progressive Christians see the book of Revelation as a picture of humans' dialectical struggle to achieve harmony with creation and reconciliation with the oneness of God (or, as some refer to as the "Self-Consciousness"). Lutheran School of Theology Professor Barbara Rossing writes,

Revelation calls us to "come out" of the beast's realm of violence and injustice so that we can participate in the beloved city of God. That call . . . is the key to Revelation's ethical imperative. The book wants us to follow the Lamb in a life-changing exodus.[28]

Theological Arguments of Biblical Christianity

The Bible refers to the Second Coming of Jesus 329 times. That should tell us how important it is. Simply put, the Second Coming brings to completion Jesus's saving work. He will return and restore all things, as He promised (Acts 3:21).

The late theologian J. Dwight Pentecost said plainly of the Second Coming: "Redemption will have been accomplished and sovereignty will have been manifested on earth."[29]

Presented below are the top ten prophetic events biblical Christians believe will unfold literally (although some aspects and interpretations of such future events are openly debated).

- Jesus will unexpectedly appear in the sky and take His Church up to Heaven (referred to as the "blessed hope," Titus 2:13), at which point Christians will be translated into their resurrected bodies (John 14:1–3; 1 Corinthians 15:51–55; 2 Corinthians 5:2–4; 1 Thessalonians 4:13–18), appear before the Judgment Seat of Christ (Romans 14:10; 1 Corinthians 3:9–15; 2 Corinthians 5:10), and celebrate the Marriage Supper with Jesus, the Lamb of God (Revelation 19:6–8).
- The Antichrist will rise to power and make peace with Israel, starting the seven-year Tribulation period (Daniel 9:24–27).

- Revelation 4:1–19:21 gives a chronological account of the Tribulation, telling of unprecedented and horrific events that will befall the world.
- At the end of the seven-year Tribulation, the Antichrist will lead an army against God at the battle of Armageddon (Revelation 19:11–21), where Jesus will quickly defeat Him upon His return and cast Him into the Lake of Fire along with Satan (Revelation 20:1–3).
- When Jesus returns, He will judge the nations and their representatives (Joel 3; Matthew 25:1–46) and rule the earth (Psalm 2:9; Isaiah 11:4).
- Israel will inhabit their land and experience the Abrahamic blessing as promised in Genesis 17 (see Amos 9:15; Ezekiel 34:28).
- Jesus's Millennial Kingdom will be marked by material and spiritual blessings; the curse upon the earth will be removed (Romans 8:19–21).
- Satan will be released after the Millennial reign and will deceive the world one last time before the New Heavens and New Earth are put in place (Revelation 20:7–10).
- The second resurrection of the wicked will occur at the Great White Throne Judgment. This is the final judgment in which those who rejected Jesus will be sentenced to the Lake of Fire (Revelation 20:11–15).
- The final consummating event will occur when God restores humanity and the world, ushering in the New Heavens and New Earth with New Jerusalem as its capital, and the entirety of creation will be filled with the glory of God (Isaiah 34:4; 65:17; 2 Peter 3:13; Revelation 21–22; Habakkuk 2:14).

Spiritual Results of Progressive Christianity

A progressive Massachusetts pastor named Matt Carriker expressed his belief in the Second Coming this way:

> Jesus came to lift us up and show us our own divinity. He came to show us that we too have the Christ potential within ourselves. The only difference between Jesus and us is that Jesus manifested the Christ potential. Many of us have not. Yet still, the Christ lies within us, waiting to be born and expressed. . . . I believe that the second coming is the coming of the Christ into our own mind, heart, and consciousness. This is what it means to be "reborn." Once in our lives are we born into our physical bodies. But when the consciousness of the Christ is born in our hearts and minds, then are we born into our spiritual bodies.[30]

Progressives focus not so much on the Son of Man's Second Coming, but on getting God's people to reconnect with Him by finding their divinity within themselves. They do not believe in a future day when Jesus Christ Himself will put an end to sin and sorrow and restore His creation to its original design. Rather, they look within themselves and rely on whatever "God" or "Jesus" means to them to bring balance and harmony to the future world.

Spiritual Results of Biblical Christianity

Our hope lies in the certainty of Jesus's return. We wholeheartedly believe the day will come when Jesus will restore His creation to its original state—and us as well. The promise of Ephesians 1:10 will be realized: "to unite all things in him, things in heaven and things on earth."

John gives us these anticipatory promises:

[Jesus] will wipe away every tear from their eyes, and death shall be no more, neither shall there be mourning, nor crying, nor pain anymore, for the former things have passed away. (Revelation 21:4)

No longer will there be anything accursed, but the throne of God and of the Lamb will be in it, and his servants will worship him. (Revelation 22:3)

For those who believe in a literal return of Jesus, keep looking up! As you do, plead for Him to "Come quickly" in great adoration and anticipation. (Revelation 22:17)

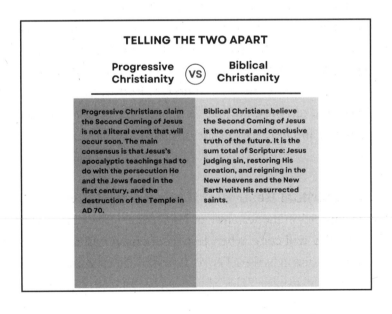

TELLING THE TWO APART

Progressive Christianity (VS) **Biblical Christianity**

Progressive Christianity	Biblical Christianity
Progressive Christians claim the Second Coming of Jesus is not a literal event that will occur soon. The main consensus is that Jesus's apocalyptic teachings had to do with the persecution He and the Jews faced in the first century, and the destruction of the Temple in AD 70.	Biblical Christians believe the Second Coming of Jesus is the central and conclusive truth of the future. It is the sum total of Scripture: Jesus judging sin, restoring His creation, and reigning in the New Heavens and the New Earth with His resurrected saints.

Key Points to Use When Talking
to Progressive Christians

Since progressive Christians deny the physical resurrection of Jesus, it makes sense that they do not anticipate Him physically returning in the future. Therefore, hold fast to these four truths when engaging with them about the eschatological hope His physical return brings.

- **Historical:** Overwhelmingly, the New Testament writers believed and taught that Jesus would personally and physically return to Earth, something many Church fathers accepted and expounded on: *The Epistle of Barnabas*, Papias (AD 60–130), Justin Martyr (AD 100–165), Irenaeus (AD 125–202), Tertullian (AD 160–220/25), Methodius (AD 250–311).
- **Biblical:** The Second Coming of Jesus is clearly outlined in the Scripture (Matthew 24–25; Mark 13; Luke 21; Acts 1:9–11; 1 Thessalonians 5:2; and Revelation 19:11–22:11).
- **Theological:** The study of end-time prophecy sheds light on every other doctrine in the Bible. It brings to completion our confident expectation that Jesus will return and restore all things as He promised (Acts 3:21). We anticipate with great fervor that the prophetic timeline of future events covered in considerable detail in the New Testament will come to pass as promised, and that Jesus Christ will physically return one day to Earth and put everything back in order.
- **Spiritual:** Jesus Christ will end sin, sorrow, death, and pain when He returns, and we will dwell in the New Heaven and New Earth for all eternity with Him.

PART 3

THREE REINVENTED

IMAGES OF JESUS

Considering progressive Christianity rejects Jesus as God, the question follows: Who is Jesus to progressive Christians? They hold strikingly different images of Him. Part Three delivers in-depth rebuttals to each one, respectively.

Jesus, the Jewish Mystic

It is no secret that progressive Christians adore many of the traditional symbols and traditions of ancient Christianity. However, they
profusely reject "the Protestant status quo" of making Jesus out to be
a tortured soul who died an atrocious death on the cross as a payment
for our sins. They find that view of Him shamefully dreadful.

Just as Jesus challenged the religious leaders of His day and
attempted to reform Judaism, so too, say progressive Christians,
are we to challenge the "rigid truths" of fundamental Christianity,
retrieve Jesus, and restore His authentic portrait to make Christianity
more relevant in the culture today.

They love to pick the four canonical gospels apart and make it
seem as if each author is describing a different Jesus.

> Each presentation of Jesus in the gospels is distinctive,
> offering a Jesus who speaks differently depending on what
> we might need him to say. Sometimes it is a Markan Jesus

who speaks to us; other times it is a Matthean or a Lukan or a Johannine Jesus. Sometimes the gospels don't speak as clearly to us, and so we might turn to innovative presentations of Jesus in art, songs, poems, or films.[1]

From this perspective, you can see how the person of Jesus can become anything to anyone at any given moment.

Therefore, many progressives, make Him out to be the "Cosmic Christ" or the "Messianic Consciousness" manifested in creation, who acts as an instrument to improve religious people's bodies, souls, and minds.

Reconstructing Jesus as an Enlightened Teacher

Marcus Borg, in his widely publicized book *Jesus*, highlights Jesus's Jewish background and argues this gave Him a greater ability to experience God.

> I suggest that, broadly understood, the term mystic designates the kind of person Jesus was—someone who experienced God vividly and whose way of seeing and life were changed as result. *What most shaped Jesus was the Jewish tradition and his mystical experience of God* [emphasis added]. He was, I argue, a *Jewish mystic* [emphasis added].[2]

Former reverend Jeffrey Frantz defines "mystic" as follows:

> For mystics, the knowing of God and the sacred is deeply personal. It is notably subjective. Each person is on a journey into the wonder and mystery of God and the sacred. For the mystic, God is found in the depths of life–working

in and through the being of this world—where all creation is called into the transcendence that reveals the depths of our humanity.[3]

Progressives say Jesus, the mystical teacher, was festooned with noble titles to exploit His image among the pagan and polytheistic cultures.[4]

Jesus Amplified as an Apocalyptic Teacher

Borg avows that Jesus was not just a mystic, but also an apocalyptic teacher who "attempted to reform Judaism. Not establish a new religion. . . . [His] disciples would later incorporate prophetic teachings to Jesus and made him into a prophet-like character who fulfilled prophecy."[5]

As a Jewish mystic, progressives say, Jesus holds authority over the Christian purview—but they consider authority to be the ethical principles in nature. They don't believe He had divine authority over nature itself.

As a gifted mystic, Jesus had a unique ability to tap into a form of persuasive power or energy that made a profound impression on the Jewish people during His time on Earth.

Jesus, a Mystical Sage

Other progressive Christians embrace a transcendent aspect of Jesus that touches on the spiritual and the holy. To them, Jesus is the "messianic consciousness"; He achieved a highly intelligent level of divine qualities that we also should strive to practice in our daily lives.

No one argues for the mystical Jesus better than John Shelby Spong. In *The Fourth Gospel: Tales of a Jewish Mystic*, he unravels the forgotten dimensions of consciousness practiced in the first century, specifically addressed in John's gospel. Although Spong believes the Nicene Creed distorted the actual image of Jesus, he thinks Jesus's teachings leave evidence of mysticism.

> Jesus, in this Jewish sense, was the place where God once again came to "tabernacle" with God's people. Jesus was the place where the human and the divine flowed together as one, so that Jesus could be heard as speaking with the voice of God. Jesus could be heard as saying that the oneness with God that he offered would satisfy the deepest human hunger and quench the deepest human thirst. In John's mind it was by relating a person to this understanding of God that a person was introduced to life that is eternal.[6]

In a chapter called "John the Non-Literalist," Spong brazenly asserts that the Gospel of John "is not about God becoming human, about God putting on flesh and masquerading as a human being; it is about the divine appearing in the human and calling the human to a new understanding of what divinity means."[7]

According to Spong, Jesus's mystical teachings act as a "doorway" into a new universal consciousness that transcends the limits of literalism and materialism, allowing us to experience all it means to be human.

The mystical mindset, progressives say, constitutes a new level of thinking, seeing, and doing. In other words, Jesus's mystical mind was highly intuitive, and the Sermon on the Mount (Matthew 5–7) are enlightened teachings that pave the way for us to experience His same transformative powers as we find our identity in the "Self-Consciousness."

Why Mystical Jesus Is a Counterfeit

The Christian mystic Adyashanti (Adya for short) is the author of *Resurrecting Jesus: Embodying the Spirit of a Revolutionary Mystic.* He writes,

> When I read the Gospels, something in me deeply connected with Jesus the revolutionary mystic, the one who is actually courageous enough to move through life guided and inspired by the dynamic of his spiritual essence. . . . Seeing Jesus through the lens of the spiritual revolutionary is powerfully transformative; if we can embody that spirit within ourselves, we can begin to break down the internal walls that separate ourselves from each other, from the world, and from our own divinity.[8]

Cynthia Bourgeault—a modern mystic, Episcopal priest, and author of *Wisdom Jesus*— praises Adya for genuinely comprehending the enlightenment of Jesus. In the foreword, she writes,

> It gives me great joy to see that in recent years some of the best books on Jesus have been written by those outside the Christian tradition, whose mature spiritual insight has allowed them to pierce through some of those intricate theological webs in which we have attempted to pin him down and package him exclusively for ourselves.[9]

I recently read those quotes to a friend who is a pastor. He said, "You see, Jason, that's what's so tricky about progressive Christianity. Take out the mystical jargon, and, to be honest, I tend to lean in that direction."

What he meant was that he *knew* Adya was conveying an unbiblical Jesus, but recognized how alluring the progressives' poetic and spiritual language can be. It seems they are talking about an intimately engaging relationship they share with the oneness of God, as though they are letting you in on a little secret that no one else was smart enough to discover on their own.

Christian mystics lace their teachings with partial truths. But that is how false teachings often work. They pique a Christian's interest by giving them a tad of biblical truth to lure them through the door. Once they are into the mystical room, many people never leave.

Which explains why it is difficult (sometimes) for the average Christian to pigeonhole progressive Christians. The "Richard Rohr types" simultaneously subscribe to progressive Christianity and Christian mysticism—leading some to wonder: *Is progressive Christianity basically Christian mysticism?*

Yes and no.

Remember that progressive Christians believe truth is (more or less) relative; therefore, the Bible is not the infallible Word of God. Therefore, if a progressive believes Christian mysticism is the spiritual path for him—that it helps him become more enlightened—then that becomes his spiritual journey and the "truth" he is living. But a different progressive Christian's path to "God" could look very different and not include embracing Jesus as a mystic.

So let us study why "Jesus, the Jewish Mystic," is a counterfeit image of Jesus by examining three false claims progressive Christians make.

False Claim #1: All Is within God, and God Is within All

Mystical progressive Christians (MPC) claim that their experiential encounters with the Absolute or "Self-Consciousness" are not primarily to gain abstract or concrete knowledge but to experience a journey to know more intimately the Absolute One-ness of the Divine.

MPCs believe our view of God (whatever you prefer "God" to be) is personal and ever-evolving. In other words, you have personal truth, and truth evolves as you become one with God, and God (he/she/it/force) becomes one with you.

Christian mystic David Benner defines a "mystic" as

> [A] person who seeks, above all else, to know God in love. Mystics are, therefore, much more defined by their longing than by their experience. They long to know God's love and thereby be filled with the very fullness of God. . . . Christian mysticism is participation in this transformational journey toward union with God in love.[10]

It is sometimes difficult to understand what MPCs are trying to say. Here are a few clarifying questions to help them get to the point.

- I realize "God" means different things to different people, but what is your definition? More to the point, what do you mean by "Absolute Oneness"?
- How can God be "Absolute Oneness" when everything is constantly changing and evolving?
- How do you know what you believe is true if truth changes with everything else in the universe?
- Where in the canonical gospels does Jesus say He is one with the universe and we, too, are to be one with the universe?
- If there is no clear distinction between God and the universe, and things are constantly in flux, how can you really know if you are pursuing God or not?

• Do you believe you possess divine qualities? If so, why?

MPCs teach that there is no distinction between God and us—implying we are all "God." Earlier, we covered what panentheism (or process theology) teaches and learned that God is not a part of the universe, nor is the universe a part of God. God is not made of matter. He is not interdependent with the world. Instead, God is above and beyond the world.

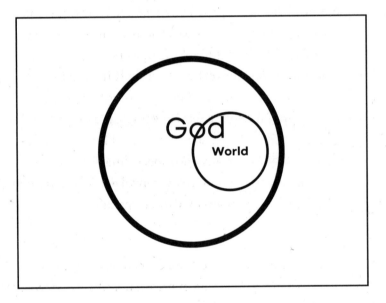

Biblical Christianity teaches that God is:

• *Simple* (absolutely one). God is not made up of parts. He is Spirit and is the Creator of the heavens and the earth (Genesis 1:1; Deuteronomy 6:4; Isaiah 40:28; Psalm 148; Hebrews 11:3).

- *Eternal.* There is no beginning or end to God. Therefore, God is separate from the universe (Deuteronomy 33:27).
- *Immutable* (unchanging). God is eternally perfect with no tendency to change (Hebrews 6:17–18). On the contrary, the universe has a beginning and is designed to change.
- *Infinite* (boundless). Everything that exists proceeds from God (Psalm 147:5; Isaiah 66:1). God does not "grow" or "improve" because He is perfect and does not conform to the nature of the universe.
- *Omnipotent* (all-powerful). God is fully capable of holding everything together by His infinite power (Exodus 6:3). Therefore, everything outside of God depends on Him for existence because He has existed for all eternity. God transcends space, time, and matter; He is immanently and intimately involved *in* and *with* His creation, but is not *one* with His creation.

Let us move on to what many MPCs believe about trinitarian doctrine. They believe it is a deep expression and reflection of the wonder of God, revealing hidden truths of our inner selves. The Trinity is a mystery but makes us more aware of becoming one with and partaking in our divinity. It is a pathway to spiritual enlightenment and wholeness.

Simply put, this is blasphemous. Only God the Father, Jesus, and the Holy Spirit are God, not us.

Trinitarian doctrine is an essential Christian teaching about the nature of God. It teaches that the Godhead is a plurality of Persons

(Father, Son, and Holy Spirit) united in one eternal essence. Many Scriptures discuss the Godhead:

- The Father is God (Romans 1:7) and a Person (Matthew 6:32)
- Jesus is God (Mark 2:5) and a Person (John 2:25)
- The Holy Spirit is God (Acts 5:3–4) and a Person (John 14:26)
- Godhead (Matthew 3:15–17; 28:19–20; 1 Corinthians 12:4–6; 2 Corinthians 13:14)

The truth is that MPCs cannot *really* know if their view of Jesus is valid if it keeps changing. Moreover, if it keeps evolving, their previous views of Jesus were clearly insufficient.

False Claim #2: Jesus Was a Jewish Mystic

MPCs and other progressive scholars consider Jesus to be the ultimate guru among other mystical figures such as Confucius, Buddha, and Lao Tzu. That is a very progressive way of saying there is no one right way to interpret Jesus. Identifying Jesus as a Jewish mystic reduces Him to being only a mortal person who made mistakes.

MPCs love to elevate Jesus's divine consciousness and appreciate His moral teachings on loving your neighbor. Deepak Chopra said the words of Jesus "ring with a truth that is very profound."[11]

Yet, no matter how much they revere Him, to progressive Christians Jesus still was only a man. They do not revere or worship Him as the Second Person of the Godhead—the Son of Man who took on a second nature, died on the cross for our sins, rose again on the third day, and is coming back to reign someday.

Apologist and philosophy professor Peter Kreeft soundly refutes such notions.

> It is utterly unhistorical to see Jesus as a mystic, a Jewish guru. . . . Jesus taught prayer, not meditation. His God is a person, not a pudding. He said he was God but not that everyone was. He taught sin and forgiveness, as no guru does. He said nothing about the "illusion" of individuality, as the mystics do.[12]

How did Jesus speak of the Heavenly Father and Himself? Did He use mystical terms and refer to Himself as a "reflection" or "habitation of the Absolute Oneness?"

Not at all.

Jesus says He is "one" (*echad*) with the Father (John 10:30–33)—affirming His divinity. He declared to the Jews that He possessed the unity of nature or equality with God. In this passage, John informs the reader that the Jews knew exactly what Jesus meant by the word "one" (*echad*) and that they were so offended by it that they picked up rocks to stone Him to death (10:31).

Thomas publicly declared Jesus to be "Lord" and "God" (John 20:28), and in Philippians 2:6, Paul describes His preexistence by saying Jesus "was in the very form God." The word "form" implies that Jesus exhibited the intrinsic nature of God—not that He "embodied" or "channeled" God-like qualities, as MPCs claim.

When Jesus took on the form of humanity, it did not subtract from His divinity, but was the addition of a second nature. Jesus, in no way, shape, or form emptied Himself of His divinity but voluntarily surrendered the free exercise of certain divine attributes while He occupied human flesh ("that though he was rich, yet for your sake he became poor" [2 Corinthians 8:9]). The emptying of Christ was only a veiling of certain transitive or relative divine attributes He chose not to reveal at certain times on Earth. It does not mean He was not God.

Moreover, when we take a closer look at the gospels, we discover three pieces of evidence for the absolute divinity of Jesus Christ: (1) prophetic fulfillment, (2) claims to be God, and (3) receiving worship as God.

1. **Jesus Christ fulfilled the Messianic prophecy** of where He would be born (Micah 5:2), that He would be of the tribe of Judah (Genesis 49:10), a descendant of King David (2 Samuel 7:16), born of a virgin (Isaiah 7:14), and would suffer and die on the cross for the sins of the world (Isaiah 53; Psalm 22).

2. **Jesus said, "I and the Father are one"** (John 10:30). The word *one* means that Christ possesses the very essence and nature of God. This is significant because only God is one, according to Deuteronomy 6:4. Furthermore, Jesus said, "Before Abraham was, I AM" (John 8:58). This was a direct claim of His eternality and Self-Existence, which was precisely what God said about Himself in Exodus 3:14.

3. **Thomas cried to Jesus, "My Lord and my God"** (John 20:28). Not only did Jesus receive worship on this occasion, but He did so without ever rebuking His followers on many other occasions throughout His Galilean ministry (see Matthew 8:2; 9:18; 14:33; 15:25).

Many MPCs look to Marvin Meyer's *The Gnostic Gospels of Jesus: The Definitive Collection of Mystical Gospels and Secret*

Books about Jesus of Nazareth as a reputable source to prove their version of Jesus as a Jewish mystic.

However, the Gnostic Gospel's case holds no weight against the veracity of the canonical gospels. Gnostic writings contradict the canonical gospels and were written hundreds of years later. Besides, no reputable Church father who affirmed the canonicity of Scripture recognized or accepted the legitimacy of Gnostic writings about Jesus.

New Testament scholar Craig Blomberg points out that the Nag Hammadi documents (mostly Gnostic writings)

> make no pretense of overlapping with the gospel traditions of Jesus' earthly life . . . a number claim to record conversations of the resurrected Jesus with various disciples, but this setting is usually little more than an artificial framework for imparting Gnostic doctrine.[13]

False Claim #3: The Kingdom of God Is within You

Luke 17:20–21 records a time when the Pharisees challenged Jesus about when the Kingdom of God would come. Jesus answered,

> "The kingdom of God is not coming in ways that can be observed, nor will they say, 'Look, here it is!' or 'There!' for behold, the kingdom of God is in the midst of you."

MPCs love to cite this passage because they believe it points specifically to the mysticism of Jesus. They interpret the Kingdom of God being "in the midst of you" to mean we are all moving toward ultimate reality or "Self-Consciousness."

Here are a few responses to debunk that idea.

First, MPCs misrepresent what Jesus said. They quote Jesus saying the "kingdom of God is *in* you." However, that is not what the original Greek word used in this passage—*entos*—means. It means "within, among, in the midst." Jesus said, "the kingdom of God is in the *midst* [emphasis added] of you" (ESV) or "the kingdom of God is *among* [emphasis added] you." Both the ESV and NASB are correct.

Second, the way Jesus answered the Pharisees would have evoked a response from them because they would have known Jesus's prophetic language sprang from Isaiah 45:14, "Surely God is in you, and there is no other, no god besides him." Jesus, as a monotheistic Jew, believed in Yahweh, a personal and transcendent Creator. Hence, Jesus did not believe God shared His glory or Being with anyone or anything else. God's Spirit is in His people, but His nature is not intrinsically united with our natural beings. Therefore, Jesus is not saying we are all one in God.

Third, Jesus was telling the Pharisees that the Kingdom of God would not appear physically and visibly as they believed it would.

Before this encounter with the Pharisees, Jesus said in Luke 11:20 that when He used His authority to cast out demons, the people would know, "the kingdom of God has come to you." Jesus was merely pointing out that God's power was present.

Moreover, since the disciples believed the Kingdom was at hand, Jesus spoke to them in parables to dispel any belief that it lay in the immediate future (Luke 19:11–27).

Fourth, MPCs seek to make a passage from the Gospel of Thomas align with Luke 17:21. It quotes Jesus saying something to the effect of, "If your leaders say to you, 'Look, the (Father's) kingdom is in the sky,' then the birds of the sky will precede you. If they say to you, 'It is in the sea,' then the fish will precede you. Rather, the (Father's) kingdom is within you and it is outside you."[14]

Once again, most reputable New Testament scholars would not put the Gospel of Thomas on the same level as the Synoptic Gospels. It lacks the structural form of Jesus's life, teachings, death, and resurrection that is found in the gospel narratives. Thomas may allude to specific passages in the New Testament, but at its core, it highlights polytheistic beliefs—a corrupt teaching that the Bible condemns.

CHAPTER 10

Jesus, the Woke
Teacher

After a recent lecture I delivered on progressive Christianity in California, a couple got in line to ask me questions.

"We enjoyed your talk on the dangers of progressive teachings in the Church," the wife said. "We are hoping you can offer us some insight about a podcast our daughter and her husband recommended we listen to."

"I'd love to help," I said curiously. "What's the name of the podcast?"

The husband reached into his pocket and pulled out his phone. "It's this one," he said, frustration in his voice. "The sermons are from GracePointe Church in Nashville, Tennessee."

I was getting different vibes from the two of them, so I gingerly asked, "Am I right in sensing there's a bit of tension between the two of you about this podcast?"

"That church is not preaching the Gospel, and our daughter is falling for their lies!" the husband shouted. The wife said she wasn't sure what to think about it.

"I am very aware of this podcast," I told them, "and can honestly say to you both that GracePointe is a progressive Christian church that prides itself in teaching Jesus as a 'Woke Teacher' who embraces all religions and celebrates LGBTQ+ people."[1]

Rebranding Jesus as Woke

I felt for that couple. Like so many, they are caught in the spiritual turmoil "woke" Christianity brings. *Merriam-Webster* defines "woke" as "aware of and actively attentive to important societal facts and issues (especially issues of racial and social justice)."[2] By that, Jesus would be the archetype of wokeness.

But that is not the full extent of how progressive Christians define it. Some would consider *Merriam's* definition a little weak.[3] They more readily embrace a "woke ideology" that supports diversity, including same-sex marriage, transgenderism, and all the various aspects of Critical Race Theory (CRT). With this brush, some progressive Christians paint Jesus as a rebel figure who didn't condemn people for their sins but was inclusive no matter what their sexual orientation or identity might be.

Through the years, many professing Christians have "come out" to endorse and support unrepentant homosexuals at all levels of church life, unequivocally stating that Jesus celebrated LGBTQ+ people in His ministry—including Tony Campolo, a famous Baptist pastor and former spiritual advisor to President Bill Clinton.

In 2015, Campolo made a blog post titled "For the Record," which stated (in part):

> It has taken countless hours of prayer, study, conversation
> and emotional turmoil to bring me to the place where I am

finally ready to call for the full acceptance of Christian gay couples into the Church.

One reason I am changing my position on this issue is that, through Peggy, I have come to know so many gay Christian couples whose relationships work in much the same way as our own.

I have concluded that sexual orientation is almost never a choice and I have seen how damaging it can be to try to "cure" someone from being gay.[4]

That view is common among progressive Christians. Their line of argument usually sounds like:

I struggled for years to reconcile the Bible's teachings on homo-sexuality with what I saw my LGBTQ+ friends and family members going through. I couldn't shake the feeling that the old ways of evan-gelicalism just weren't cutting it anymore. Gradually, my beliefs and opinions changed to support LGBTQ+, eventually leading me to look at Scripture differently to back up my newfound progressive beliefs. I look at their LGBTQ+ friends and family and think, *How can their lives be a sin when all I see is love?*

Many younger progressive Christians have told me they have changed their minds about Jesus through inclusive teachings because it made His image more loving and palatable. Jen, a twenty-five-year-old who attends an inclusive church, told me, "It's almost like the inclusive Christians have freed Jesus from all the things the traditional church has taught He is against. When I affirm people of all walks of life, I am loving them the way Jesus would have loved them."

I asked Jen if she had ever read *The Divine Romance* by Richard Rohr. At the mention of his name, her face beamed with excitement.

"Of course I've read that book! It really opened my eyes to a deeper love of Jesus."

In that book, Rohr wrote that Jesus "ignores, denies, or openly opposes his own Scriptures whenever they are imperialistic, punitive, exclusionary, or tribal."[5]

Campolo, Jen, and countless others have exchanged the Word of God for the *words and feelings* of man.

Rohr's quote about Jesus "opposing his own Scriptures" if they are not inclusive enough exposes this progressive tactic: Eliminate or repurpose anything that opposes the inclusive ethics and woke standards of progressive Christianity.

In a widely read *New York Times* article, Peter Wehner chastised ancient and modern Christians for neglecting to teach just how inclusive Jesus is.

> First-century Christians weren't prepared for what a truly radical and radically inclusive figure Jesus was, and neither are today's Christians. We want to tame and domesticate who he was, but Jesus' life and ministry don't really allow for it. He shattered barrier after barrier.[6]

Prominent voices in progressive Christianity, including Jen Hatmaker, John Pavlovitz, Chris Seay, David Gushee, Jonathan Merritt, Colby Martin, Guthrie Graves-Fitzsimmons, and Rob Bell, say the vitriol with which the Church has treated LGBTQ+ people has provoked many to steer clear from the stained-glass Jesus taught and cherished in conservative Sunday schools. It is high time, they say, to liberate Jesus and usher in a new gospel of inclusivity that celebrates same-sex marriage, equality for sexual orientation, and equity for minorities and the poor. In the same way that Jesus challenged the status quo in His day, so must we stand up for same-sex marriage and those exiled from churches because Christians told them homosexuality was a sin.[7]

Progressive Christians appeal to the "woke" ideology they say Jesus personified when He preached against the elites of His day. When Jesus called Matthew the tax collector to join Him, visited the Samaritan woman, and ate at the house of the despised Zacchaeus, He was identifying Himself as a "Woke Teacher."

This wokeness is on full display at ProgressiveChristianity.org.

In an article titled, "If Jesus Were Alive Today . . . ," the writer presumes to speak on His behalf by glaringly writing that Jesus would be

> in the street marching with his brothers and sisters for health care and a living wage. He would be raising his voice and his fist on behalf of those who claim the right to marry regardless of gender. He would be raising his voice and his fist on behalf of an earth already dealing with the ravages of climate change, with fires that consume entire states, continents that are melting, hurricanes that wash away cities and towns. . . . [He would] march with those who protest against racial injustice, not with those who protest against the wearing of masks. He would seek a middle ground between respect for the life of the unborn and the life of those who actually give birth. He would be a "terrorist" pulling down the statue of a confederate general because people who fought their countrymen for the right to keep slaves should not for that reason be honored in the public square.[8]

In addition, progressive Christians like to make "traditional Christians" seem like patriarchal, xenophobic, homophobic, transphobic white supremacists and exclusivists. One of them is David Gushee, a famous writer, ethicist, and pastor.

In his bestselling book, *After Evangelicalism: The Path to a New Christianity*, Gushee writes that Jesus

> carries himself with great intimacy with God. He has profound spiritual power. He exercises that power on behalf of others, those who need it most. He is against legalism and for an understanding of his Abba Father that leads to human welcome, healing, acceptance, and love. His teachings are authoritative, rooted in his Jewish tradition and picking up the robust global inclusivity that is part of an eschatological strand of that tradition. This is a Jesus who knows that his calling is going to lead to his quick and terrible death in Jerusalem.[9]

Gushee stresses that Jesus's "robust global inclusivity" was too much for the exclusivist Pharisees to handle, so they had Him killed for heresy. This is exactly how progressive Christians see themselves against biblical Christians. They like to point out that they are called "heretics" for being inclusive or reimagining the Bible.[10] Because Jesus was challenged, persecuted, and even sentenced to death, they wear the "heretic" label as a badge of honor. To them, being a heretic means being like Jesus. When encountering that label, they will often ask if you're using it "For loving people? For feeding the poor? For befriending the outcasts of society just like Jesus did?"

This and similar tactics can all be found in the books below:

- *Just Faith: Reclaiming Progressive Christianity* (Guthrie Graves-Fitzsimmons)
- *The Shift: Surviving and Thriving after Moving from Conservative to Progressive Christianity* (Colby Martin)

- *Before You Lose Your Mind: Deconstructing Bad Theology in the Church* (Keith Giles)
- *Christianity in Blue: How the Bible, History, Philosophy, and Theology Shape Progressive Identity* (David Kaden)
- *Jesus and John Wayne: How White Evangelicals Corrupted a Faith and Fractured a Nation* (Kristin Kobes Du Mez)

Why "Jesus, the Woke Teacher" Is a Counterfeit

Remember how the Gay/Inclusive Gospel found its way into many evangelical circles?

"Woke Jesus" is using the same channels. It is meant to sway the masses to believe in a sympathetic, Savior-like figure who approves

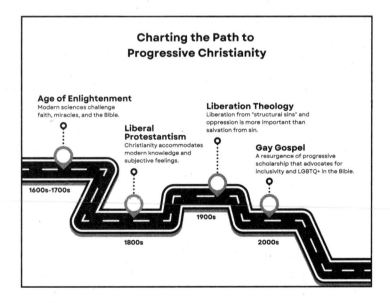

Charting the Path to Progressive Christianity

Age of Enlightenment
Modern sciences challenge faith, miracles, and the Bible.

1600s-1700s

Liberal Protestantism
Christianity accommodates modern knowledge and subjective feelings.

1800s

Liberation Theology
Liberation from "structural sins" and oppression is more important than salvation from sin.

1900s

Gay Gospel
A resurgence of progressive scholarship that advocates for inclusivity and LGBTQ+ in the Bible.

2000s

of your personal beliefs and behaviors. It is almost like believing in a "Santa Claus Jesus" who gives you whatever you want as long as you believe you have been "good for inclusivity's sake."

How does one combat that theology?

First Response: Jesus Is Not the "Ground of Being" but the Supreme Being over Everything

In her book *Freeing Jesus*, progressive theologian Diana Butler Bass employs mystical titles given to Jesus by other liberal and progressive Christians (Paul Tillich, Richard Rohr, Ilia Delio, Matthew Fox, and Rowan Williams) to establish Him as an inclusive teacher, including the "Cosmic Christ," the "Ground of Being," the "Heart of Creation," and the "Universal Christ."

> This is the truth of Jesus. That Jesus—the one known intimately as friend and teacher, experienced as Savior and Lord, who guides on the way and inhabits the ordinary—is also the universal Jesus, the welcoming and inclusive Jesus, the Jesus of the circle and in the circle, the all in all.[11]

I am sure you have noticed by now that most progressive Christians diminish Jesus's divinity by making Him out to be a "superhero" or "liberator," or by blending Him into creation as merely a manifestation of "God"—representing their panentheistic worldview.

I love what Stand to Reason founder Greg Koukl has written about how progressive Christians love to twist Scripture or throw out passages that do not align with their worldview.

> Here's the real issue. We have one body of detailed information about Jesus: the canonical Gospels. We can accept them as divinely inspired or not. We can accept them (as

many scholars do) as non-inspired human documents that are, on the main, historically accurate. We can even accept them as error-ridden musings by primitive people about God and Jesus. What we cannot do, though, is reject the Gospel accounts out of hand and then advance our own personal opinion of the Jesus of the Gospels, since there will be no Jesus left to have a personal opinion about. Reject the record, and you forfeit your opinion of the man of the record. It's that simple. Of course, if you cherry-pick verses to fashion a Jesus in your own image, then I have nothing to offer you. If that's your project, you are welcome to your fantasy, but do not mistake the views of your make-me-up Christ for the views of Jesus of Nazareth. That legend will reflect your opinions, not his.[12]

We read in the Holy Bible that Jesus is the Uncaused First Cause. That is, Jesus is not a sum of creation; He is the Creator who created the universe. Christ exists endlessly and depends on no one for His existence because He is the Supreme Being (see John 1:1–3; Colossians 1:16–17).

The writer of Hebrews said this about Jesus:

> But in these last days he has spoken to us by his Son, whom he appointed the *heir of all things*, through whom also he created the world. He is the *radiance of the glory of God and the exact imprint of his nature*, and he *upholds the universe by the word of his power*. After making *purification for sin*s, he sat down at the *right hand of the Majesty on high*, having become as much *superior to angels* as the name he has inherited is *more excellent* than theirs. (1:2–4; emphasis added)

Here the writer lays out the divine authority of Jesus as the Son of God. First, Jesus is the "heir of all things," a reference to His prominence in Heaven and supremacy over the universe. Second, Jesus "created the world"—a phrase that points to Jesus's existence before time, space, and matter were created. Third, Jesus is the "radiance of the glory of God." The word used for *radiance* means "reflection; the shining forth." It means Jesus is the very splendor and glory of God. Fourth, Jesus is the "exact imprint of his nature (substance)." Building on the descriptive language of "radiance," the writer presents Jesus as the exact representation of God. Fifth, Jesus "upholds the universe," marking Him as the Sustainer of all things. Sixth, Jesus "atoned for sins" and is at the "right hand of the Majesty on high." Jesus is our Redeemer, our great High Priest, who defeated sin and death and is exalted in Heaven in glorious majesty. And seventh, Jesus is "much superior to angels." No mighty creature can compare to Jesus Christ, and none is His equal (see Ephesians 1:21; Philippians 2:9).

Second Response: Jesus's Teachings Were Exclusive

Be careful not to fall for progressive Christians' "love talk." This is when they make it sound like Jesus loved everyone for who they are and what they believe to be true for them. There was never any judgment from Him, no talk of "go and sin no more"—only love and affirmation.

The progressive Christians below paint Jesus with this rainbow brush of inclusivity:

- Rachel Held Evans
- Jen Hatmaker
- Rob Bell
- Derek Webb (former lead singer of Caedmon's Call)
- Brian McLaren

- Michael and Lisa Gungor
- Brandan Robertson[13]

But Jesus was not a moral teacher who advanced a harmonious message embracing all points of view branded by "inclusivity" or the "gay rainbow." Progressive Christians fail to realize that throughout Jesus's ministry, He taught against sinful behavior and was known for openly rebuking those who were leading people astray. Jesus taught against many false views prominent in His day, especially when it came to the religiosity of the Sanhedrin—so much so that many of Jesus's critics accused Him of being demon-possessed (Mark 3:22).

John Mark records Jesus saying,

> "For from within, out of the heart of man, come evil thoughts, sexual immorality, theft, murder, adultery, coveting, wickedness, deceit, sensuality, envy, slander, pride, foolishness. All these evil things come from within, and they defile a person." (Mark 7:21–23)

After calling out sins, Jesus would often point to Himself as the *only* One who could offer forgiveness.

> "I told you that you would die in your sins, for unless you believe that I am he you will die in your sins." (John 8:24)

That does not sound like an "all-accepting" Jesus who endorses every opinion and celebrates a wide variety of perversions.

Jesus, who is Love, is also Truth. He loves every human being because they are created in His image. But that is not the same as loving their every thought, belief, or deed.

Progressive Christians are hard pressed to find passages in the canonical gospels of Jesus discussing other paths that lead to God. He said in John 14:6, "I am the Way, and the Truth, and the Life. No one comes to the Father except through Me." Notice the two truths presented here. On the one hand, Jesus's statement is *inclusive* in the sense that He came to die for every person—not just one person or a particular race or class. However, the other truth is that it is an *exclusive* offer of eternal life—meaning no other person or religious pathway outside of Jesus Christ can offer it to you.

So, yes, Jesus is *inclusive* in that His death made salvation possible for everybody, but He is also *exclusive* in that it is only through Him one can be saved and receive everlasting life.

Jesus is *the way*. Every other path leads to dead ends.

Jesus is *the truth*. Every other search leads to false answers.

Jesus is *the life*. Every other promise leads to hopeless fates.

Third Response: Our Identity Is in Jesus Christ, Not in Anything Else

Sometimes the things progressive Christians say go well into offensive territory. For me—and probably for you as well—former evangelical pastor Chris Kratzer is one of the most egregious. I apologize in advance for this excerpt from his book, *Stupid Sh*t Heard in Church*.

Here's a message you probably won't hear at church this morning—the greatest problem and threat to your life isn't sin. I repeat, it's not sin. Not even close. Rather, it's the false gospel within much of American Christianity that mixes Love with conditions. It mixes Grace with an angry, vengeful God. One who loves people so much that He tortures them eternally if they don't love Him back in return, and Jesus with a conservative, white, sexist, racist, male, heterosexual privilege, bigotry, and nationalism. The only card Satan can and desires to play in your life is condemnation, convincing you that God, you, and other people are less; less loved, whole, good, valued, and affirmed. In fact, here's the gospel of conservative, Evangelical Christianity . . . "Everything is wrong with you, and you need to believe and become like us in order to fix it, or else." Now, here's the Gospel of Grace through Jesus . . . "Nothing is wrong with you. You are already completely like, as, and in full communion and union with Jesus. You are whole, righteous, pure, loved, affirmed, saved, lacking no spiritual blessing, and without any condemnation whatsoever for your life." One promises to bring you "life" only to bring you a life of living death. The other is Life through and through, from beginning to end; freely, thoroughly, and unconditionally given to you.[14]

I agree that fundamentalism and legalism in evangelicalism have misled people to wrongly believe they need to conform to their rituals and bow to their sacred cows. But guess what? That is not Christianity. And progressive Christians like Kratzer know it.

Here is a question I want you to be aware of when conversing with a progressive Christian: If sin is not the problem, as Kratzer says, what do you call people who use religion to abuse people?

The question reveals a double standard.

Denying that we are sinful while pointing out the sin of others is not only hypocritical, but judgmental. It's easy to make it seem as if Christianity is untrue if all you are doing is pointing out the flaws, mistakes, sins, and wrongdoings of church leaders. Anyone can attempt to discredit Christianity by taking samples from prosperity preachers—or any celebrity pastor flaunting their expensive shoes on stage. But those people, despite their flaws, do not in any way discredit Christianity itself.

Let us get more to the point: We are the Imago Dei. We are made in our Maker's image, signifying God's imprint on our lives spiritually, morally, physically, and intellectually. And God, in His original creation, made everything perfect.

Tragically, the image of God was effaced from us at the Fall in the Garden of Eden. Nevertheless, in His great love, the Father sent His Son to take on flesh and die on the cross for our sins, so that His image can be restored in us and we can be adopted into His heavenly family.

However, Kratzer not only rejects the notion that we are born in sin, he rejects the necessity of the atonement of Jesus Christ.

So then, how can you have progressive Christians who are "righteous, pure, loved, saved," and yet simultaneously label biblical Christians as sexist, racist, fundamentalists, etc.? How is Kratzer justifying one camp to be righteous while the other is not? What is his standard, and where does it come from if he rejects sin and Jesus as Savior?

The answer to this conundrum is found in the words of Paul:

> I have been crucified in Christ. It is no longer I who live, but Christ who lives in me. And the life I now live in the flesh I live by faith in the Son of God, who loved me and gave himself for me. (Galatians 2:20)

The compound verb for "crucified" (*sustauroō*) is in the perfect tense of a completed action with lifelong effects. The Bible teaches that we are "buried with (Jesus) by baptism into death" and "raised to walk in newness of life" (Romans 6:4).

Elsewhere, Paul writes that we "have put on the new self, which is being renewed in knowledge after the image of its creator"

(Colossians 3:10). Paul is saying that our new life and identity is in union with Christ and is constantly being renewed as we become more like Him.

Jesus not only loves us perfectly; He defines us. Our identity is not based on the world's standards or on our own philosophy. As believers in Jesus Christ, our identity encompasses all the abundance of being beloved children of God.[15]

Fourth Response: Jesus Called Out Sin and Affirmed Natural Marriage between a Man and a Woman

One popular argument progressive Christians make is that Jesus never mentioned homosexuality and, therefore, has been mistakenly viewed as someone who condemned LGBTQ+ people.

The late American preacher and progressive theologian Peter Gomes (1942–2011) goes so far as to say that if Christians don't change their views on sexuality (specifically homosexuality), we are denying the authority of Scripture.

> The battle for the Bible, of which homosexuality is the last front, is really the battle for the prevailing culture, of which the Bible itself is a mere trophy and icon. Such a cadre of cultural conservatives would rather defend their ideology in the name of the authority of scripture than concede that their self-serving reading of that scripture might just be wrong, and that both the Bible and the God who inspires it may be more gracious, just and inclusive than they can presently afford to be.[16]

For progressives like Gomes, to believe homosexuality is a sin and to affirm that marriage is only between a man and a woman is virtually disavowing God as a gracious and loving Being.

It should be pointed out that, as followers of Jesus Christ, we must treat each person with dignity and respect. We are called to love people, including our enemies, as Jesus taught (see Matthew 5:43–48). However, that does not mean we are to love everything they stand for. People are prone to tell lies and believe they are true. This is precisely the reason we help them see the truth: because we love them. So, if progressive Christians want to use Jesus as their benchmark, then let us see what He taught and how He spoke the truth.

First, Jesus did not need to actively campaign against homosexuality. In the first century, the Jewish people knew that same-sex relations was not morally permissible. In fact, it was prohibited.

Second, as a Jewish rabbi, Jesus obeyed and followed the Law. When a lawyer challenged Him about the greatest commandment, Jesus responded by citing from the Mosaic Law (see Matthew 22:34–40). More to the point, if Jesus had been asked point blank if homosexuality were a sin, He would have turned to Leviticus 18:22 and 20:13 to plainly show that the Scriptures condemn homosexual practices as sinful before God.

Third, when the Pharisees challenged Him about divorce, Jesus deliberately anchored His response to the normative Genesis account that marriage is between a man and a woman. You will only find Jesus affirming marriage between a man and a woman. Therefore, it is a stretch for progressive Christians to say He supports same-sex marriage, because He never did!

Fourth, read Matthew 15:10–20 to your progressive Christian friend and ask if he agrees that any of the sins Jesus mentions are, in fact, sins. If that person accepts some but not all of those things as sins, they disagree with Jesus and are essentially calling Him a liar.

Progressive Christians cannot have it both ways: They cannot say Jesus affirmed same-sex marriage when there is no evidence He did while rejecting what He did say about sin.

Fifth, Paul, who believed in Jesus and avidly followed His teachings, referred to homosexuality as an unnatural activity. This perspective very much aligns with the teachings of Jesus in Matthew 5:27–31 (sexual sin and divorce), Matthew 12:33–37 (a tree is known by its fruit), Matthew 15:10–20 (how is a person defiled), and Matthew 19:4–9 (marriage and sexual immorality). The term Paul uses in Romans 1:26–27 and 1 Timothy 1:10 is derived from two words: *arsēn* (man) and *koitē* (bed). Combining the two words, you get *arsenokoitai*, found in the Septuagint (Leviticus 18:22; 20:13). By examining these four passages, it is clear that the Bible precisely judges homosexuality to be "unnatural" and a sin.

However, Matthew Vines, an openly gay man who professes to be a conservative Christian, likes to point out that Romans 1 is addressing what he calls "unrestrained lust," "pagan religion," and "idolatry," and has nothing to do with a person's sexual orientation. In so doing, he makes several mistakes.

One, he is inserting something into the text that is not there. Paul is not saying homosexuality is only a sin if it becomes an idol. He is calling it out as an "unnatural" proclivity/act that violates God's divine design for humanity and marriage.

Two, Vines inserts his radical view of what it means to be human into the passage. According to him, sexuality or orientation is a strong attribute of one's identity. This flies in the face of what the Bible teaches about human nature and sexuality per God's design.

Third, Vines attempts to discredit Paul's apostolic authority by audaciously claiming that he was naive about sexual orientation—as if Paul did not realize that some people are born that way. Once more, it is a stretch on Vines's part.

Dr. Anthony Thiselton provides an exceptional response to Paul's message regarding sexual immorality.

What is clear from the connection between 1 Cor 6:9 and Rom 1:26–29 and their OT backgrounds is Paul's endorsement of the view that idolatry, i.e., placing human autonomy to construct one's values above covenant commitments to God, leads to a collapse of moral values in a kind of domino effect.[17]

Speaking the Truth in Love

I encourage you not to get sucked into the drama progressive Christians often stage. They will call you homophobic for believing what the Bible literally teaches about homosexuality. They will say you are misguided, brainwashed, or even ignorant. That's fine. Let them mock you. You are not called to *appease* them; you are called to *please* the Lord!

I close out this chapter with a powerful message from a former lesbian and radical leftist professor, Rosaria Butterfield—now a committed follower of Jesus Christ.

When Jen Hatmaker began publicly supporting the LGBTQ+ community and branding an inclusive gospel in her posts and books, Butterfield wrote:

To be clear, I was not converted out of homosexuality. I was converted out of unbelief. I didn't swap out a lifestyle. I died to a life I loved. Conversion to Christ made me face the question squarely: did my lesbianism reflect who I am (which is what I believed in 1999), or did my lesbianism distort who I am through the fall of Adam? I learned through conversion that when something feels right and good and real and necessary—but stands against God's Word—this reveals the particular way Adam's sin marks my life. Our sin natures deceive us. Sin's deception isn't just "out there"; it's also deep in the caverns of our hearts.

How I feel does not tell me who I am. Only God can tell me who I am, because he made me and takes care of me. He tells me that we are all born as male and female image bearers with souls that will last forever and gendered bodies that will either suffer eternally in hell or be glorified in the New Jerusalem. Genesis 1:27 tells me that there are ethical consequences and boundaries to being born male and female.[18]

To show someone you love them is to speak the truth to them with love—even when that means letting them know what they believe is false and can harm them. But the good news is, Jesus offers them forgiveness and desires reconciliation with them.

Jesus didn't convey through His messages or His miracles that He is one of many Ways by which we can reach peace with God. Jesus presented Himself as the One and the only True God—*the* Way, *the* Truth, and *the* Life. As Erwin Lutzer said,

If He is the truth, He is the truth for everyone. Whether one accepts Christ or not is a separate question, but He is either the truth for all or the truth for none.[19]

So, the loving thing to do is show progressive Christians what Jesus's love is and what it stands for—and present to them the *real* portrait of Jesus Christ so delightfully revealed in the pages of Scripture.

CHAPTER 11

Jesus, the
Revolutionist

The world did not know it, but trudging through the humble streets of Nazareth was a revolutionist who would turn the world upside down in a matter of decades.

Though a peasant with limited education and no influential backing, this Jew, who went by the name of Jesus, would eventually become the most recognizable Jewish orator of the millennium, whose teachings would rock the imperialistic Roman regime to its core and beyond.

This is the image of Jesus painted by another class of progressive Christians.

Religion professor R. David Kaylor speaks of Jesus as a political leader who attempted to overthrow the elites of Judaism in the first century.

> I do believe that Jesus preached and taught a message that
> was thoroughly political, a message that demanded a social

or political revolution. If Jesus had his way, the current ruling elites would no longer remain in their positions of power, or if they did, they would rule in a very different manner. In that sense he was political.[1]

How much of what Kaylor reports about Jesus is true? Is any of it true? Was Jesus's mission on Earth more political and social than we believe? There is an activist side of progressive Christianity that parades Jesus as a revolutionary mascot who resembles Che Guevara, Gandhi, and, to some degree, the Communist leader Vladimir Lenin. It is similar to Jesus, the Woke Teacher, but more aggressively political.

So let us now turn our attention to how a segment of progressive Christians have turned Jesus into a revolutionary figure whose life was cut short by insurrection—leaving His disciples to devise a movement that would eventually come to venerate Him as the Son of God.

Revolutionizing Jesus's Mission

Southern Methodist University Professor Brad R. Braxton argues that Christianity needs to be more about expanding a revised message of Jesus for the future than expounding on what He did in the past.

In his explosive article, "Getting in Front of Jesus: The Politics of Progressive Christianity," Braxton announces that

[T]hose of us who bear Jesus' name should creatively replicate Jesus' progressive stance. Following Jesus requires us to turn our faces as much to the present and future as to the past. The good news of the gospel is progressively unfolding itself and inviting us to proceed with faith and flexibility, instead of an unyielding set of narrowly defined, rigid doctrines.[2]

This directive is not original to Braxton. He credits the progressive theologian James Forbes, who insists that Jesus was a progressive and "was open to having his understanding of truth and love broadened."[3]

Postmodern theologian Peter Rollings likes to think of Jesus as a trickster. In an interview with *The Atlantic*, he said,

> Tricksters are revolutionary figures that challenge the natural order. They poke holes in what everyone takes for granted and fight systems that oppress. They work within a given religious or political system, but they wrestle with it, challenge it and transform it. In Jesus, we see a trickster figure, one who respects the beliefs and traditions of real people, yet also questions them, challenges them and *subverts them for the sake of political and religious transformation.* [emphasis added][4]

In Rollings's opinion, Jesus was not the Savior of the world, but a revolutionist who was compelled to fight against the oppression of His day and bring about social reform.

Pastor Dawn, a self-proclaiming "21st Century Progressive Christian Pastor," agrees.

> Jesus practiced a non-violent resistance in ways that impacted his people and worried his oppressors. Jesus knew God as LOVE and proclaimed that LOVE, even going so far as to teach people to LOVE their enemies. Jesus challenged the religious authorities of his day to see beyond the scriptures and embody the God which he defined as LOVE. Jesus claimed ONEness with God and called upon his followers to understand their own ONEness with one

another. Jesus was anything but a pacifist. Jesus was an activist, an agitator who practiced civil disobedience in ways which got him noticed by the oppressive powers of empire. Jesus refused to avoid confrontation with those very powers. Jesus was political, always speaking out on behalf of the poor and the marginalized. Jesus threatened the status quo. Jesus threatened the economic system because it oppressed the poor and enslaved the wealthy. Jesus threatened the military might of the Roman Empire because of the needless suffering and death which was all around him. Jesus taught a Way of being in the world which encouraged his followers to live life abundantly, and to love extravagantly, pointing to a God who is LOVE.[5]

Much of what you have read about this counterfeit Jesus is due largely to the influence of John Dominic Crossan.

Crossan is one of the most influential and leading thinkers in the Jesus Seminar and has written extensively on Jesus as a revolutionary cynic. In his most distinguishable book, *Jesus: A Revolutionary Biography*, Crossan conjures up the idea that Jesus was like pagan cynics, who were dissenters who did not back down from the social order of their day.

Pagan Cynicism involved practice and not just theory, lifestyle and not just mindset, in opposition to the cultural heart of Mediterranean civilization—a way of looking and dressing, of eating, living, and relating that announced its contempt for honor and shame . . .

Jesus and his first followers fit very well against that background; they were hippies in a world of Augustan yuppies.[6]

Why "Jesus, the Revolutionist" Is a Counterfeit

Let's examine three bogus claims that reside in the counterfeit image of "Jesus, the Revolutionist."

Bogus Claim #1: Jesus Led a Revolution to Break the Bondage of Oppressive Religion

There is some truth to this claim. However, like so many of the claims progressive Christians make, it is not grounded on the Bible's infallibility. It omits the idea that Jesus came to save sinners. Therefore, the focal point is not Jesus as "Savior" but Jesus as a "Liberator" who personified an inordinate amount of conviction and great resolve to do the right thing as He fought for the marginalized and motivated a generation to carry on His legacy.

N. T. Wright's comprehensive book, *Jesus and the Victory of God*, lists a few liberal views of Him during the Second Temple era. For example, American Bible scholar G. W. Buchanan (1921–2019) believed Jesus was hoping for a violent revolt during His lifetime but settled on building support for one to arrive in the future.[7] Richard A. Horsley, a retired professor of religion, believed Jesus belonged to a society of nonviolent peasants who supported the rise and power of local bandits and helped initiate certain violent measures to "oppose the system that had systematically brutalized them."[8]

While there certainly was an undercurrent of revolution among Jews during the Second-Temple era—especially the Zealots—Jesus never sought to start a revolution. That idea is found nowhere in the gospel narratives. There is no evidence of Jesus in any way siding with a movement seeking to overthrow Rome or to push out the Sanhedrin.

Certainly, Jesus confronted the religious leaders of His day and spoke truth to power. But it's a stretch to take Jesus "turning over tables" as an act of revolution that sparked the flame that led to the Jewish Revolt in AD 66–70.

What did Jesus do in John 6:15, when a group of people were seeking to make Him king by force? Did He let them? Did He stir the crowd and set off an insurgency to take over as ruler?

Nope.

The end of John 6:15 says He "withdrew again to the mountain by himself." If He had been forging a band of rebels, that definitely was a missed opportunity.

When two of Jesus's disciples, James and John—thinking He was about to initiate an insurrection—asked Him to give them prominent positions, Jesus responded that to go high means to go low. "Even the Son of man came not to be served but to serve, and to give his life as a ransom for many" (Mark 10:45). That does not sound like a revolution, does it? (Maybe a revolutionary way to go about serving others!)

When Jesus dined with Zacchaeus in Jericho, He told the other guests, "The Son of Man came to seek and to save the lost." Was He talking about a revolution? Not at all.

The context is Zacchaeus was feeling guilty for robbing the people and repents of his greed. In response, Jesus says to him, "Today salvation has come to this house" (Luke 19:9).

Jesus came into the world to save sinners—not start a revolution or launch a coup.

Matthew 1:21 tells us an angel appeared to Joseph in a dream and told him that Mary would give birth to a son, "and you shall call his name Jesus, for he will save his people from their sins."

The word "sins" does not mean "oppressive regimes." It is the Greek word *hamartia* (ἁμαρτία), "to act contrary to God's will or law; to miss the mark; to engage in wrongdoing."

When Jesus embarked on His public ministry in Galilee, He announced, "The time is fulfilled, and the kingdom of God is at hand; repent and believe in the gospel" (Mark 1:15). He says nothing about a revolution.

If anything, the revolution Jesus created was for people to repent of their sins and believe in Him as the Messiah, the promised One. That sounds more like a revival of souls than it does a revolution seeking political power.

Later in Luke 4:43 and 8:1, Jesus defined the "kingdom of God" not as an insurrection but as "proclaiming the good news." In the Garden of Gethsemane, after Peter cut off Malchus's ear (see Luke 22:49–51; John 18:10–11), Jesus said,

> "Put your sword back into its place. For all who take the sword will perish by the sword. Do you think that I cannot appeal to my Father, and he will at once send me more than twelve legions of angels? But how then should the Scriptures be fulfilled, that it must be so?" (Matthew 26:52–54)

Jesus then turned to the crowd and said,

> "Have you come out as against a robber, with swords and clubs to capture me? Day after day I sat in the temple teaching, and you did not seize me. But all this has taken place that the Scriptures of the prophets might be fulfilled." (Matthew 26:55–56)

Jesus scolds His disciples for behaving violently. He then adds that if He wanted to cause destruction, He could have done it quickly. At this point, Jesus proceeds to make a case for His innocence.

Did he ever commit acts of violence while teaching at the temple courts? No.

Brad R. Braxton interprets Jesus's death and resurrection as an act of justice.

> Jesus was a revolutionary. He died not of old age but met a death similar to that of his revolutionary mentor John the Baptist. When Jesus stepped into the Jordan River to be baptized, he declared allegiance to God's revolution, which meant he could not pledge allegiance to Rome's inhumane agenda. Jesus was so committed to his mission of creating communities of love and inclusion that he willingly died for it. For justice, Jesus lived and died. For justice, God raised Jesus from the dead. The resurrection serves notice that injustice—and the oppression and death it brings—will never have the last word.[9]

A progressive Christian blogger adopts a more extreme position, interpreting Jesus's death as a revolt against organized religion.

> Jesus's resurrection dramatizes the higher calling by positing a judge who stands apart from Rome and Judea and who can see Jesus the radical outsider for what he is and appreciate his vision of an ideal social order. The gospel narrative is a fantasy for marginalized people of all stripes, including introverts, radicals, hippies, bohemians, starving artists, losers, outcasts, mystics, and idiots (in Dostoevsky's sense).[10]

The bottom line is that progressive Christians dress Jesus up in the same outfit as Barabbas, completely butchering His apocalyptic teachings along the way.

Like N. T. Wright, I believe Jesus devoted some time and attention to correcting the Jews' false views and corrupt rituals. But that is not the same as suggesting He was actively trying to overthrow Rome or the Sanhedrin as a Jewish freedom fighter.

Jesus said in John 4:34 that His overarching objective on Earth was to "do the will of him [the Father] who sent me and to accomplish his work."

Ultimately, Jesus came to bring victory over sin and death and to defeat demonic principalities. Jesus not only repudiated people in power, but also reigned over the cosmic powers of Satan.

Bogus Claim #2: Jesus Stood for Social Justice

In an attempt to identify the meaning of the three temptations Satan used against Jesus, Brian Zahnd writes

> The first temptation is to feed everyone . . . and forget about God. This is the temptation to make the kingdom of God solely about social justice. Yes, Jesus will multiply loaves and fishes and feed the hungry, but he will also say, "eat my flesh and drink my blood." We cannot achieve the second commandment to love our neighbor as our self if we bypass the first commandment to love God with all our heart. The second temptation is to persuade everyone . . . and eliminate faith. This is the temptation to prove God empirically—either by miracles or by science—and thus remove the need for faith . . . The third temptation is the most subtle of all. It's the temptation to liberate everyone . . . and kill the bad guys.[11]

At first glance, what Zahnd says about the first and second commandments seems spot on. But the question we need to ask is, "What does he mean by 'social justice'?"

Zahnd does not really explain that. This is known as an equivoca-
tion fallacy: Zahnd is being ambiguous in his use of "social justice."
This can cause confusion among readers, or lead them to assume a
particular meaning the author did not intend. However, this often
happens when progressive Christians practice a form of eisegesis,
in which the interpreter undermines the real meaning of the biblical
context to support his own biased views. Nothing in the three temptations mentioned in Matthew 4:1–11 and Luke 4:1–12 has anything
to do with social justice.

A few years ago, Zahnd tweeted:

> What some call social justice Jesus called the kingdom of
> God.[12]

There's another case of eisegesis. What does Zahnd mean by
"social justice" and how does he define what Jesus said about the
Kingdom of God? It's a broad statement with no specifics to hang
your hat on.

John Pavlovitz explains social justice according to progressive
Christians as

> the heart of the Gospel, that it was the central work of
> Jesus as evidenced in his life and teachings; the checking
> of power, the healing of wounds, the care for the poor, the
> lifting of the marginalized, the feeding of the hungry, the
> making of peace.[13]

Personally—and this is where biblical Christians need to find
common ground—I believe that Zahnd and Pavlovitz see social justice
as the hands and feet of Jesus. We can agree that we are to feed and
clothe the poor, and, as James writes, "to visit orphans and widows

in their affliction" (1:27). But for progressive Christians, social justice runs much deeper than that.

If you recall, Pavlovitz and most of his like-minded contemporaries deny the miracles of Jesus. They believe He essentially went around aiding, feeding, and befriending the outcasts of society. Furthermore, Pavlovitz vehemently rejects the atonement Jesus provided on the cross for our sins. He does not see the Gospel as Jesus dying for our sins, being buried, rising again, and ascending to heaven (see 1 Corinthians 15:3–8).

One blogger summed up the progressive view on this by writing,

> But Jesus's moral radicalism—according to which the poor deserve to be rich and the rich deserve to be poor—fires the imagination of progressive Christians, inspiring their battles for social justice and for reining in the capitalism and consumerism that threaten the planet's ability to support our species.[14]

Because of this, social justice is about doing the same moral and politically charged actions Jesus did. As you commit more acts of kindness, end global warming, and rein in capitalism, you are becoming more like Jesus—which progressive Christians see as a form of salvation.

Biblical Christians readily reject this because it runs contrary to who Jesus is, what He taught, and the distinctions the New Testament makes about how we are saved not *by* good works, but *for* them (see Ephesians 2:8–9; Titus 2:11–14).

Bogus Claim #3: Jesus Was a Socialist

In her book, *Interrupted: When Jesus Wrecks Your Comfortable Christianity*, Jen Hatmaker writes that Jesus rooted for the underdog, concocted "radical economic theories," and held "revolutionary redistribution concepts."[15]

I realize she does not refer to Jesus as a "socialist," but let us not be fooled; that is what she is insinuating. What is so sad is that millions of Christians who read Hatmaker's book never thought to challenge this mischaracterization of Jesus.

No one is arguing that Jesus didn't care for the poor and needy. That was a priority for Him. But it was not the entirety of His mission on Earth, and that's how progressive Christians often make it sound.

In his study of the canonical gospels, Greg Koukl points out,

> I could not find a single sentence where Jesus championed the cause of the poor, the outsider, or the disenfranchised as such. There is not even a hint of it—in the sense that it's commonly understood—in the entire historical account of the life of Jesus of Nazareth.[16]

Foundation for Economic Education President Emeritus Lawrence W. Reed writes,

> Jesus never even implied that accumulating wealth through peaceful commerce was in any way wrong; he simply implored people to not allow wealth to rule them or corrupt their character. That's why his greatest apostle, Paul, didn't say money was evil in the famous reference in 1 Timothy 6:10. Here's what Paul actually said: "For the love of money is a root of all kinds of evil. Some people, eager for money, have wandered from the faith and pierced themselves with many griefs." Indeed, progressives them- selves have not selflessly abandoned money, for it is other

people's money, especially that of "the rich," that they're always clamoring for.[17]

So true.

Jesus never taught (even parabolically) His followers to look to the government for assistance in health care, unemployment, or to raise more taxes so their lifestyles could be subsidized by welfare.

What we actually see is Jesus rebuking a man who wants Him to convince his brother to equally distribute his wealth (see Luke 12:13–21).

In two gospel accounts, Matthew 22:15–22 and Mark 12:13–17, Jesus is challenged by polar-opposite groups as to whether paying poll-tax (tribute money) to Caesar is in accordance with the law of God. On one side were the Herodians, who endorsed the Roman policy of paying the poll-tax. On the other were the Pharisees, who sought to entrap Jesus as a lawbreaker if He sided with the Gentiles over contributing to the emperor's treasury.

Jesus does not fall for either view.

He did not stand for imperialism or socialism. Instead, He rightly distinguishes the proper rights and authority between the government ("render to Caesar what belongs to Caesar") and God ("render to God what belongs to God").

Those who attempt to pull an endorsement of socialism out of Matthew 22:15–22 and Mark 12:13–17 are clearly implanting a false version of what Jesus meant in His response to the Herodians and the Pharisees.

When Mary Magdalene anointed Jesus's feet with nard, the disciples were outraged by the waste. What did Jesus do? Did He agree with His disciples? Was He outraged, too? No. Jesus responded by directing their attention to more important things,

"For you always have the poor with you, but you will not always have me" (Matthew 26:11).

In fact, only on two occasions did Jesus mention the "poor" in association with His mission. The first is described in Luke 4:18–19, when Jesus affirms His identity as the Messiah, and the second is when He reported to John the Baptist signs of confirmation that He was the Messiah (Matthew 11:4–5). In both cases, the main objective was to bring redemption and forgiveness to the world through His death and resurrection—not to argue for socialism, reparations, or the redistribution of wealth.

Though Jesus challenged and opposed many social norms in His day, that is not to say He was a Zealot or a revolutionist. Jesus's mission was far greater than attempting to overthrow Roman imperialism. His mission carried with it eternal consequences. Jesus didn't come to bring His people political freedom or provide aid for their physical needs. He came to rescue His people from their sins and offer them eternal life. Jesus didn't come to reform religion. He came to restore souls.

That said, don't be fooled into believing this false image of Jesus. But be like Peter, who said to Jesus after many disciples stopped following Him, "You have the words of eternal life, and we have believed, and have come to know, that you are the Holy One of God" (John 6:68–69).

From Counterfeits to Encountering the True and Living Jesus

Everyone wants to add a "Jesus Approved" sticker to their way of life. But here's the ultimate question: Who is Jesus?

In the last section of this book, I presented three counterfeit versions of Jesus progressive Christians profess.

If Jesus isn't God, then He was a liar—a mystical teacher or revolutionist who deceived His followers into believing He was something more than He truly was.

If Jesus isn't God, then we are all left dead in our sins and have no way of redeeming ourselves from the penalty of eternal separation from God and damnation. There is no Kingdom of Heaven for us. No forgiveness. No healing. No hope . . . and that would make the "gospel of Jesus" the biggest Ponzi scheme the world has ever seen.

So knowing and believing that Jesus Christ is the Son of God, the Savior of the world, matters. It matters so much that the fate of every human soul depends on it.

After reading *Hijacking Jesus,* I hope you are more cognizant of the vast differences between progressive Christianity and biblical Christianity and readily able to defend the divinity of Jesus Christ, along with His virgin birth, miracles, atonement on the cross, resurrection, and His return to Earth before long.

Do not let progressive Christians sway you to "revitalize" your image of Jesus. The only way to know who He really is is to encounter Him in the pages of Scripture. My hope is that you will hold fast to the glorious truth that Jesus (the Second Person of the Godhead) took on flesh, conquered sin and death at His resurrection, and that our glorious risen Savior is King over all creation!

Know what the Bible teaches, and let its truth preserve and protect you as you defend its beauty against those who seek to hijack Jesus.

Notes

Introduction

1. Gary Dorrien, *The Making of American Liberal Theology*, vol. 1, *Imagining Progressive Religion, 1805–1900* (Louisville, Kentucky: Westminster John Knox Press, 2001). Dorrien, a professor of social ethics at Union Theological Seminary, refers to "progressive theology" as a "liberal retrieval of the symbols of the Christian tradition."

2. Borg fleshes this point out in chapter one, "Jesus Today: Telling His Story" and chapter four, "The Shaping of Jesus: Jewish Tradition in an Imperial World" in *Jesus: Uncovering the Life, Teachings, and Relevance of a Spiritual Revolutionary* (New York: HarperOne, 2015).

3. The main reason for using "biblical Christianity" instead of "evangelical Christianity" or "evangelical Protestantism" is because the term "evangelical" has a variety of meanings in the sociopolitical landscape in America.

Chapter 1: The Conspiracy to Hijack Jesus

1. Brian Zahnd, *The Unvarnished Jesus* (self-pub., 2019), 2–3, Kindle.

2. Brian D. McLaren, *The Secret Message of Jesus: Uncovering the Truth That Could Change Everything* (Nashville, Tennessee: Thomas Nelson, 2007), 3.

3. Pete Enns, "Episode 70: TGC Doesn't Really Get Progressive Christianity and Atheism," *The Bible for Normal People* (podcast), December 3, 2018, https://peteenns.com/the-tgc-doesnt-really-get-progressive-christianity-and-atheism.

4. David P. Gushee, *After Evangelicalism: The Path to a New Christianity* (Louisville, Kentucky: Westminster John Knox Press, 2020), 65, Kindle.

5. Marcion is the first of the great heretical teachers and contemporary to the gnostic teacher Valentinus of Rome.

6. J. N. D. Kelly, *Early Christian Doctrines*, rev. ed. (New York: HarperOne, 1976), 230.

7. J. Ed Komoszewski, M. James Sawyer, and Daniel B. Wallace, *Reinventing Jesus: How Contemporary Skeptics Miss the Real Jesus and Mislead Popular Culture* (Grand Rapids, Michigan: Kregel Publications, 2006), 154–55.

8. Thomas Rees, *The Racovian Catechism* (Lexington, Kentucky: The American Theological Library Association, 1962), 149.

9. As the progressive blogger Lydia Sohn puts it, "Liberal Christian theologies saw that doctrines were not timeless truths dictated by God that we had to discover, but rather revisable and historically situated cultural products of our best efforts to say something true about one's own experience of God," in "A Brief Primer on Progressive Christianity," Medium, March 23, 2018, https://medium.com/s/story/a-brief-primer-on-progressive-christianity-4f7a60c92ad8.

10. Gregory A. Boyd, *Cynic Sage or Son of God?* (Wheaton, Illinois: Victor Books, 1995), 36.

11. In his book *Studying the Historical Jesus*, Darrell Bock states that Reimarus (a Deist) believed that "Jesus in the Gospels differed from that of the apostles in the Epistles. Jesus taught and preached very much as a Jew. However, his death led the apostles to develop the idea of a suffering redeemer around him. Reimarus argued that the disciples stole Jesus' body and that a perspective arguing for an alleged resurrection had also infiltrated the Gospels, so that finding the real Jesus would take careful historical work." Darrell L. Bock, *Studying the Historical Jesus: A Guide to Sources and Methods* (Grand Rapids, Michigan: Baker Academic, 2005), 143.

12. Tillich's theology of God is on track with pantheism, and he subscribed to a Bultmannian view of antisupernaturalism.

13. Harnack built on the Ritschilian tradition—that Christianity is more about ethical living than systematized doctrines. He was also a pioneer in the Social Gospel movement.

14. Q is an unknown document that is argued to have a source which Matthew and Mark used in order to write their own gospel accounts. Friedrich Schleiermacher mistook Papias's (AD 110) writings about the "oracles" of Jesus to mean "sayings of Jesus." Q doesn't affect anything regarding the authenticity of Scripture.

15. Sanders, a strong proponent of historical-critical ideologies, believes that centuries later, the Church inserted teachings Jesus's teachings into historical accounts to reflect the Savior they wanted Him to be.

16. In *Jesus: Uncovering the Life, Teachings, and Surprising Relevance of a Spiritual Revolutionary* (1994), Borg famously recasts the Jesus of history and the Christ of faith into (1) Pre-Easter Jesus (not God) and (2) Post-Easter Jesus (God revealed to us). Borg did not believe Jesus was the Son of God who died for the sins of humanity, and said the resurrection carries metaphorical meaning.

Chapter 2: New Theology on the Block

1. Colby Martin, *The Shift: Surviving and Thriving after Moving from Conservative to Progressive Christianity* (Minneapolis: Fortress Press, 2020), 7.

2. Roger Wosley, *Kissing Fish: Christianity for People Who Don't Like Christianity* (Bloomington, Indiana: Xlibris Corp., 2011), 63.

3. Scotty McLennan, *Jesus Was a Liberal: Reclaiming Christianity for All* (New York: St. Martin's Press, 2011), viii.

4. "The Core Values of Progressive Christianity," ProgressiveChristianity.org, accessed November 15, 2022, https://progressivechristianity.org/the-8-points.

5. Progressive Christian scholars think objective viewpoints are dogmatic. That comes from Kantianism.

6. Diana Butler Bass, *Freeing Jesus: Rediscovering Jesus as Friend, Teacher, Savior, Lord, Way, and Presence* (New York: HarperOne, 2021), Introduction.

7. John Shelby Spong, *Jesus for the Non-Religious* (New York: HarperCollins, 2008), 136.

8. Ibid., 2–3.

Chapter 3: Hijacking Jesus's Divinity

1. Shawn Meyers, "Oklahoma Minister Claims Jesus Is Not God," YouTube, August 4, 2009, https://youtu.be/SJYsbJIJ2k4.

2. David M. Felten and Jeff Procter-Murphy, *Living the Questions: The Wisdom of Progressive Christianity* (New York: HarperOne, 2012), 191.

3. David A. Kaden, *Christianity in Blue: How the Bible, History, Philosophy, and Theology Shape Progressive Identity* (Minneapolis: Fortress Press, 2021), 48.

4. J. Ed Komoszewski, M. James Sawyer, and Daniel B. Wallace, *Reinventing Jesus: How Contemporary Skeptics Miss the Real Jesus and Mislead Popular Culture* (Grand Rapids, Michigan: Kregel Publications, 2006), loc. 1631–35, Kindle.

5. Quotations from Irenaeus's *Proof of the Apostolic Preaching* are taken from Joseph P. Smith, trans., *St. Irenaeus: Proof of the Apostolic Preaching* (New York: Newman Press, 1952), 78.

6. Justin Martyr, *First Apology*, trans. Alexander Roberts and James Donaldson (Logos Virtual Library), chapter 13.

7. John Shelby Spong, *Jesus for the Non-Religious* (New York: HarperCollins, 2007), 144.

8. Felten and Procter-Murphy, *Living the Questions*, 52.

9. Dale C. Allison, *The Historical Christ and the Theological Jesus* (Grand Rapids, Michigan: William B. Eerdmans Pub. Co., 2009), 84.

10. Ibid.

11. Diana Butler Bass, *Freeing Jesus: Rediscovering Jesus as Friend, Teacher, Savior, Lord, Way, and Presence* (San Francisco: HarperOne, 2021), 167–68.

12. A. T. Robertson, *Word Pictures in the New Testament* (Nashville, Tennessee: Broadman Press, 1933), John 1:1.

13. Ibid., John 20:28.

14. Murray J. Harris, *Three Crucial Questions About Jesus* (Grand Rapids, Michigan: Baker Books, 1994), 98–99.

15. John F. Walvoord, *Jesus Christ Our Lord* (Chicago: Moody Press, 1969), 144.

16. Ibid., 139.

17. Millard J. Erickson, *The World Became Flesh: A Contemporary Incarnational Christology* (Grand Rapids, Michigan: Baker Book House, 2000), 477–78.

18. John B. Cobb Jr., *The Process Perspective* (St. Louis, Missouri: Chalice Press, 2003), 39.

19. Robert Cornwall, "Why Progressive Christianity Needs Process Theology (Bruce G. Epperly)," Ponderings on a Faith Journey, October 19, 2011, https://www.bobcornwall.com/2011/10/why-progressive-christianity-needs.html.

20. Richard Rohr, *The Universal Christ: How a Forgotten Reality Can Change Everything We See, Hope For, and Believe* (New York: Convergent, 2021), 5.

21. Delwin Brown, *What Does a Progressive Christian Believe?: A Guide for the Searching, the Open, and the Curious* (New York: Seabury Books, 2008), 32–35.

22. Robert W. Funk, *Honest to Jesus: Jesus for a New Millennium* (San Francisco: HarperSanFrancisco, 1997), 63–65.

23. Walvoord, *Jesus Christ Our Lord*, 26.
24. Ibid., 188–89.
25. Ibid., 112.
26. Butler Bass, *Freeing Jesus*, 240.
27. Ibid.
28. Peter Enns, "Jesus Had a Fallen Nature, Just Like the Bible," July 9, 2012, https://peteenns.com/jesus-had-a-fallen-nature-just-like-the-bible.
29. Josh McDowell and Sean McDowell, *Evidence That Demands a Verdict: Life-Changing Truth for a Skeptical World* (Nashville, Tennessee: Thomas Nelson, 2017), 204.

Chapter 4: Hijacking Jesus's Virgin Birth

1. Chautauqua Institution, "Bishop John Shelby Spong—His Last Public Lecture," YouTube, June 28, 2018, https://www.youtube.com/watch?v=QVs3z3nxWdc.
2. Elaine Pagels, *Beyond Belief* (New York: Vintage Books, 2003); Bart Ehrman, *Jesus Before the Gospels* (New York: HarperOne, 2017).
3. John Shelby Spong, *Jesus for the Non-Religious* (New York: HarperOne, 2009), 15.
4. Joseph Campbell, a mythologist, writes in his book *The Hero with a Thousand Faces*, "[Virgin birth stories are] recounted everywhere; and with such striking uniformity of the main contours, that the early Christian missionaries were forced to think that the devil himself must be throwing up mockeries of their teaching wherever they set their hand" (p. 309).
5. Whitley Strieber, *Jesus: A New Vision* (San Antonio, Texas: Walker & Collier, Inc., 2020), 29.
6. Giles Fraser, "The Story of the Virgin Birth Runs against the Grain of Christianity," *The Guardian*, December 24, 2015, https://www.theguardian.com/commentisfree/2015/dec/24/story-virgin-birth-christianity-mary-sex-femininity.
7. Ed Taylor, "Affirmations and Confessions of a Progressive Christian Layman – Mary and Joseph," ProgressiveChristianity.org, December 13, 2013, https://progressivechristianity.org/resources/affirmations-and-confessions-of-a-progressive-christian-layman-mary-and-joseph.
8. Melito, in *Discourse on the Cross*: "On these accounts He came to us; on these accounts, though He was incorporeal, He formed for Himself a body after our fashion—appearing as a sheep, yet still remaining the Shepherd; being esteemed a servant, yet not renouncing the Sonship; being carried in the womb of Mary, yet arrayed in the nature of His Father; treading upon the earth, yet filling heaven; appearing as an infant, yet not discarding the eternity of His nature; being invested with a body, yet not circumscribing the unmixed simplicity of His Godhead; being esteemed poor, yet not divested of His riches; needing sustenance inasmuch as He was man, yet not ceasing to feed the entire world inasmuch as He is God; putting on the likeness of a servant, yet not impairing the likeness of His Father. He sustained every character belonging to Him in an

immutable nature: He was standing before Pilate, and at the same time was sitting with His Father; He was nailed upon the tree, and yet was the Lord of all things."

9. Tertullian, *The Ante-Nicene Fathers: Fathers of the Third and Fourth Century*, vol. 3, *Latin Christianity*, eds. Arthur Cleveland Cox, James Donaldson, and Alexander Roberts (New York: Cosimo Classics, n.d.), 756.

10. J. Warner Wallace, "Did the 'Virgin Conception' First Appear Late in History?," Cold Case Christianity, December 7, 2018, https://coldcasechristianity.com/writings/did-the-virgin-conception-first-appear-late-in-history.

11. You can find Origen's rebuttal here, "Celsus as quoted by Origen," Early Christian Writings, http://www.earlychristianwritings.com/text/celsus.html.

12. James F. McGrath, "Was Jesus Illegitimate? The Evidence of His Social Interactions," *Journal for the Study of the Historical Jesus* 5, no. 1 (2007): 81–100, https://doi.org/10.1177/1476869006074937.

13. J. Ed Komoszewski, M. James Sawyer, and Daniel B. Wallace, *Reinventing Jesus: How Contemporary Skeptics Miss the Real Jesus and Mislead Popular Culture* (Grand Rapids, Michigan: Kregel Publications, 2006), 260.

14. Helpful resources that debunk parallelism: Leon McKenzie, *Pagan Resurrection Myths and the Resurrection of Jesus* and Ronald Nash, *The Gospel and the Greeks*.

15. Marcus J. Borg, *Jesus: Uncovering the Life, Teachings, and Surprising Relevance of a Spiritual Revolutionary* (New York: HarperCollins, 2006), 60–61.

16. Robin R. Meyers, *Saving Jesus from the Church: How to Stop Worshiping Christ and Start Following Jesus* (New York: HarperCollins, 2010), 40–41.

17. Jonathan M. S. Pearce, "Debunking the Nativity: The Mistranslation of 'Virgin,'" Patheos, December 7, 2016, https://www.patheos.com/blogs/tippling/2016/12/07/debunking-nativity-mistranslation-virgin/.

18. Meyers, *Saving Jesus from the Church*, 41.

19. David M. Felten and Jeff Procter-Murphy, *Living the Questions: The Wisdom of Progressive Christianity* (New York: HarperOne, 2012), 181–82.

20. Mark L. Strauss, *Four Portraits, One Jesus: A Survey of Jesus and the Gospels*, 2nd ed. (Grand Rapids, Michigan: Zondervan Academic, 2020), 317.

21. Ibid., 271.

22. *The Lexham Bible Dictionary* (Bellingham, Washington: Lexham Press, 2016), s.v. "virgin."

23. M. S. Mills, *The Life of Christ: A Study Guide to the Gospel Record* (Dallas, Texas: 3E Ministries, 1999).

24. Ibid.

25. Luke Wayne, "Did Paul Deny the Virgin Birth?," Christian Apologetics and Research Ministry, December 5, 2018, https://carm.org/about-bible-verses/did-paul-deny-the-virgin-birth.

26. James D. Tabor, *Jesus Dynasty: The Hidden History of Jesus, His Royal Family, and the Birth of Christianity* (New York: Simon & Schuster, 2007), 59.
27. Spong, *Jesus for the Non-Religious*, 15.
28. Felten and Procter-Murphy, *Living the Questions*, 191.
29. John Calvin, *The Institutes of the Christian Religion*, trans. Henry Beveridge (Orange, Connecticut: Samizdat Express, 1845), 733.
30. Peter Lewis, *The Glory of Christ* (Carlisle, England: Paternoster Press, 1997), 134.
31. Delwin Brown, *What Does a Progressive Christian Believe?: A Guide for the Searching, the Open, and the Curious* (New York: Seabury Books, 2008), 37.
32. David A. Kaden, *Christianity in Blue: How the Bible, History, Philosophy, and Theology Shape Progressive Identity* (Minneapolis: Fortress Press, 2021), 166.
33. Elliot Ritzema, ed., *300 Quotations and Prayers for Christmas* (Bellingham, Washington: Lexham Press, 2013).

Chapter 5: Hijacking Jesus's Miracles

1. See chapter seven, "Fish Stories," in Rachel Held Evans, *Inspired: Slaying Giants, Walking on Water, and Loving the Bible Again* (Nashville, Tennessee: Nelson Books, 2018).
2. Paula Fredriksen, *Jesus of Nazareth, King of the Jews* (New York: Vintage Books, 1999), 112–13.
3. Ed Taylor, "Affirmations and Confessions by a Progressive Christian Layman – Jesus' Miracles," ProgressiveChristianity.org, February 3, 2014, https:// progressivechristianity.org/resources/affirmations-and-confessions-by -a-progressive-christian-layman-jesus-miracles-by-ed-taylor.
4. Fredriksen, *Jesus of Nazareth, King of the Jews*, 115.
5. See Craig S. Keener, *Miracles: The Credibility of the New Testament Accounts*, vol. 1, chapter 2, "Ancient Miracle Claims outside Christianity."
6. Craig S. Keener, *Miracles: The Credibility of the New Testament Accounts*, vol. 1 (Grand Rapids, Michigan: Baker Academic, 2011), 124.
7. Rudolf Bultmann, *Jesus and the Word* (Tübingen, Germany: Mohr, 1926), 146 (as quoted by Jarl Fossum, "Understanding Jesus' Miracles," *Bible Review* 10, no. 2 [April 1994]: 23).
8. Richard A. Horsley, *Jesus and Magic: Freeing the Gospel Stories from Modern Misconceptions* (Eugene, Oregon: Cascade Books, 2014), 62.
9. S. Vernon McCasland, "Signs and Wonders," *Journal of Biblical Literature* 76, no. 2 (June 1957): 149–52, https://doi.org/10.2307/3261285.
10. Craig L. Blomberg, "The Miracles as Parables," *Gospel Perspectives* 6 (1986): 327–59; see also Craig L. Blomberg, *The Historical Reliability of the Gospels* (Downers Grove, Illinois: InterVarsity Press, 1987), 130–34.
11. See H. E. G. Paulus, *The Life of Jesus as the Basis of a Purely Historical Account of Early Christianity* (1828); David F. Strauss, *The Life of Jesus, Critically Examined* (1835–1836); Albert Schweitzer, *The Quest of the Historical Jesus* (1906).

12. David Friedrich Strauss, *The Life of Jesus, Critically Examined* (New York: Calvin Blanchard, 1860), 39–43, 87–91.

13. John Shelby Spong, *Jesus for the Non-Religious* (New York: HarperOne, 2009), 50–51.

14. Ibid., 51.

15. Ibid., 93.

16. Ibid.

17. Dale C. Allison, *The Historical Christ and the Theological Jesus* (Grand Rapids, Michigan: William B. Eerdmans Pub. Co., 2009), chapter 3.

18. Taylor, "Affirmations and Confessions by a Progressive Christian Layman – Jesus' Miracles."

19. Ibid.

20. Paula Fredriksen, *From Jesus to Christ: The Origins of the New Testament Images of Christ*, 2nd ed. (New Haven, Connecticut: Yale University Press, 1988), 99.

21. Mark's gospel treats miracles as symbolic demonstrations of the kingdom of God rather than validations of Jesus and the Gospel (Vernon K. Robbins, "*Dynameis* and *Semeia* in Mark," *Biblical Research* 18 [1973]: 1–16; compare Mark R. Saucy, "Miracles and Jesus' Proclamation of the Kingdom of God," *Bibliotheca Sacra* 153, no. 611 [July 1996]: 281–307). Matthew's gospel uses miracles to portray Jesus as the fulfillment of God's promise to raise up a prophet like Moses (Deuteronomy 18:18; Wayne Baxter, "Mosaic Imagery in the Gospel of Matthew," *Trinity Journal* 20, no. 1 [Spring 1999]: 76). Luke's gospel and Acts refer to the miracles of Jesus and the early Christ-followers as validating signs and wonders (e.g., Acts 2:43; Paul Achtemeier, "The Lucan Perspective on the Miracles of Jesus," *Journal of Biblical Literature* 94, no. 4 [December 1975]: 553–56; G. W. H. Lampe, "Miracles in the Acts of the Apostles," 165 in *Miracles: Cambridge Studies in Their Philosophy and History*, ed. C. F. D. Moule [London: Mowbray, 1965]). Miracles in Acts work within a mutually interpretative relationship with the Gospel message (Daniel Marguerat, *Magic and Miracle in the Acts of the Apostles* [T&T Clark, 2004], 124). John's gospel describes Jesus's miracles as explanatory signs (σημεῖα, *sēmeia*); the text never calls them "miracles" (δύναμεις, *dynameis*; Howard Clark Kee, *Medicine, Miracle, and Magic in New Testament Times* [Cambridge: Cambridge University Press, 1988], 88; *Lexham Bible Dictionary* [Bellingham, Washington: Lexham Press, 2016], s.v. "miracle.")

22. N. T. Wright, *Jesus and the Victory of God*, vol. 2 (Minneapolis: Fortress Press, 1996), 188.

23. M. G. Easton, *Illustrated Bible Dictionary and Treasury of Biblical History, Biography, Geography, Doctrine, and Literature* (New York: Harper & Brothers, 1893), 468.

24. Robin Keeley, ed., *Nelson's Introduction to the Christian Faith* (Nashville, Tennessee: Thomas Nelson, 1995), 64.

25. Rudolf Bultmann, *The New Testament and Mythology and Other Basic Writings*, trans. and ed. Schubert M. Ogden (Philadelphia: Fortress Press, 1984), loc. 96–98, Kindle.

26. Spong, *Jesus for the Non-Religious*, 54–55.

27. Scotty McLennan, *Jesus Was a Liberal: Reclaiming Christianity for All* (New York: St. Martin's Press, 2009), 125.

28. Ibid., 60, 125.

29. Sarah Bessey, *Jesus Feminist: An Invitation to Revisit the Bible's View of Women* (Nashville, Tennessee: Howard Books, 2013), 149.

30. Keener, *Miracles*, 243.

31. The Laws of Nature relate to the natural world. They are not physical entities that comprise properties that *cause* events to happen or *describe* the normalcy of nature based on regular past experiences (what uniformly happens).

32. Keener, *Miracles,* 98.

33. Tawa J. Anderson, W. Michael Clark, and David K. Naugle, *An Introduction to Christian Worldview: Pursuing God's Perspective in a Pluralistic World* (Downers Grove, Illinois: InterVarsity Press, 2017), 164.

34. Rob Bell, *What We Talk about When We Talk about God* (New York: HarperOne, 2014), 79.

35. Jarl Fossum, "Understanding Jesus' Miracles," *Bible Review* 10, no. 2 (April 1994): 17.

36. Ibid.

37. John Pavlovitz, *If God Is Love, Don't Be a Jerk: Finding a Faith That Makes Us Better Humans* (Louisville, Kentucky: Westminster John Knox Press, 2021), 31.

Chapter 6: Hijacking Jesus's Atonement

1. Dawn Hutchings, "Time to Vaccinate Ourselves against the Infection of Atonement Theology," ProgressiveChristianity.org, April 2, 2021, https://progressivechristianity.org/resources/time-to-vaccinate-ourselves-against-the-infection-of-atonement-theology.

2. Stephen Prothero, *American Jesus: How the Son of God Became a National Icon* (New York: Farrar, Straus and Giroux, 2003), 83–84.

3. Marcus J. Borg, *Meeting Jesus Again for the First Time: The Historical Jesus and the Heart of Contemporary Faith* (New York: HarperCollins, 1994), 26.

4. Megan Bailey, "Jesus Did Not Die on the Cross for Our Sins," Beliefnet, July 27, 2022, https://www.beliefnet.com/faiths/christianity/jesus-did-not-die-on-the-cross-for-our-sins.aspx.

5. Marcus Borg, "The Real Meanings of the Cross," Patheos, October 28, 2013, https://www.patheos.com/blogs/marcusborg/2013/10/the-real-meanings-of-the-cross.

6. Doug Pagitt, *A Christianity Worth Believing: Hope-Filled, Open-Armed, Alive-and-Well Faith for the Left Out, Left Behind, and Let Down in Us All* (San Francisco: Jossey-Bass, 2009), 181.

7. "Atonement," Theopedia: An Encyclopedia of Biblical Christianity, accessed October 3, 2022, https://www.theopedia.com/atonement.

8. Alister E. McGrath, *Studies in Doctrine* (Grand Rapids, Michigan: Zondervan, 1997), 100. McGrath writes, "While Jews celebrated their deliverance by God from Egypt by eating a lamb, Christians would henceforth celebrate their deliverance by God from sin by eating bread and drinking wine. Passover celebrates the great acts of God by which the people of Israel came into being; the Eucharist celebrates the great act of God by which the Christian church came into being."

9. Jesus dying on the cross for our sins and rising from the dead was an early and most common doctrinal belief among Christians in the book of Acts (see 2:32; 3:15, 26; 4:10; 5:30; 10:40; 13:30, 33–34, 37; 17:31; 26:23).

10. See John R. Stott, *The Cross of Christ* (Downers Grove, Illinois: InterVarsity Press, 1986), 21.

11. Gregory Boyd, "The 'Christus Victor' View of the Atonement," ReKnew, November 29, 2018, https://reknew.org/2018/11/the-christus-victor-view-of-the-atonement.

12. See chapter 10, "Love and Wrath as Consent," in Bradley Jersak, *A More Christlike God: A More Beautiful Gospel* (Pasadena, California: Plain Truth Ministries, 2015).

13. Rob Bell, *What Is the Bible?: How an Ancient Library of Poems, Letters, and Stories Can Transform the Way You Think and Feel about Everything* (New York: HarperOne, 2019), 241.

14. Rob Bell, *The Gods Aren't Angry* (San Francisco: Zondervan Publishing, 2008), DVD.

15. See chapter 6, "Blood on the Doorposts of the Universe," in Rob Bell and Don Golden, *Jesus Wants to Save Christians: Learning to Read a Dangerous Book* (New York: HarperOne, 2012).

16. Joel B. Green, ed., *Dictionary of Jesus and the Gospels: A Compendium of Contemporary Biblical Scholarship*, 2nd ed. (Downers Grove, Illinois: InterVarsity Press, 2013), 179.

17. The *Dictionary of Jesus and the Gospels* illuminates the meaning of the Passover meal with greater insight into the Old Testament: "Jesus uses the elements of the meal (bread, cup, wine) to interpret his impending death. Jesus sees his death as inaugurating the new covenant foretold in Jeremiah's promise (Jer 31:31–34) that one day God would restore Israel from exile. Luke's phrase 'covenant in my blood' probably alludes to Exodus 24:8, with the result that Jesus' new covenantal sacrifice enables people to participate in the eschatological new-covenant relationship with God promised in Jeremiah 31:31–34" (p. 186).

18. Kenneth S. Wuest, *Wuest's Word Studies from the Greek New Testament for the English Reader*, vol. 2 (Grand Rapids: Eerdmans, 1997), 80.

19. William Paul Young, *Lies We Believe about God* (New York: Atria Books, 2017), 149.

20. Lou Kavar, "A Progressive Christian Minister Reconsiders Atonement," *Emerging Spirituality Weekly* (blog), April 5, 2017, https://blog.loukavar.com/2017/04/05/a-progressive-christian-minister-reconsiders-atonement.

21. Donald Schmidt, *Death of Jesus for Progressive Christians: A Five Session Study Guide* (Kelowna, Canada: Wood Lake Publishing, 2019), 99.

22. Nicholas Kristof, "Reverend, You Say the Virgin Birth Is 'a Bizarre Claim'?," *New York Times*, April 20, 2019, https://www.nytimes.com/2019/04/20/opinion/sunday/christian-easter-serene-jones.html.

23. Schmidt, *Death of Jesus for Progressive Christians*, 99.

24. David M. Felten and Jeff Procter-Murphy, *Living the Questions: The Wisdom of Progressive Christianity* (New York: HarperOne, 2012), 118.

25. Marcus J. Borg, *Jesus: The Uncovering the Life, Teachings, and Surprising Relevance of a Spiritual Revolutionary* (New York: HarperCollins, 2006), 269.

26. Richard Rohr, *The Universal Christ: How a Forgotten Reality Can Change Everything We See, Hope For, and Believe* (New York: Convergent, 2021), chapter 12.

27. Tony Jones, *Did God Kill Jesus?: Searching for Love in History's Most Famous Execution* (New York: HarperOne, 2015), 20.

28. Tony Jones, *A Better Atonement: Beyond the Depraved Doctrine of Original Sin* (Minneapolis: The JoPa Group, 2012), Interlude.

29. Norman L. Geisler, *Systematic Theology, Volume Three: Sin, Salvation* (Minneapolis: Bethany House Publishers, 2004), 202.

30. *Lexham Theological Wordbook* (Bellingham, Washington: Lexham Press, 2014), s.v. "atonement."

31. William Lane Craig, *Atonement and the Death of Christ an Exegetical, Historical, and Philosophical Exploration* (Waco, Texas: Baylor University Press, 2020), 125.

32. Ibid., 77.

33. Millard J. Erickson, *Christian Theology* (Grand Rapids, Michigan: Baker Books, 1984), 782.

34. See chapter one, "Jesus the Teacher, Not the Savior," in Robin Meyers, *Saving Jesus from the Church: How to Stop Worshiping Christ and Start Following Jesus* (New York: HarperCollins Publishers Inc., 2010).

35. John Shelby Spong, *Jesus for the Non-Religious* (New York: HarperOne, 2009), 4.

Chapter 7: Hijacking Jesus's Resurrection

1. Peter Kreeft and Ronald K. Tacelli, *Handbook of Christian Apologetics: Hundreds of Answers to Crucial Questions* (Downers Grove, Illinois: InterVarsity Press, 1994), 176.

2. Michael Green, *Man Alive!* (Downers Grove, Illinois: InterVarsity Press, 1968), 61.

3. Pitt Street Uniting Church, "Saving Jesus from the Church – Rev Robin Meyers PhD – 20-05-2016," YouTube, May 21, 2016, https://www.youtube.com/watch?v=cnfJcZkZ2OU&ab_channel=PittStreetUnitingChurch.

4. Paula Fredriksen, *From Jesus to Christ: The Origins of the New Testament Images of Jesus* (New Haven: Yale University Press, 1988), 125–26.

5. Richard Bauckham, *Jesus and the Eyewitnesses: The Gospels as Eyewitness Testimony* (Grand Rapids, Michigan: William B. Eerdmans Pub. Co., 2006), 7.

6. John Oakes, "Which of the Four Gospels Was Written First?," Evidence for Christianity, September 8, 2017, https://evidenceforchristianity.org/which-of-the-four-gospels-was-written-first/.

7. Dr. Norm Geisler and Dr. Frank Turek write, "This date also makes sense in light of Paul's quotation of Luke's gospel. Writing sometime between AD 62–65, Paul quotes from Luke 10:7 and calls it 'Scripture' (1 Tim. 5:18). Therefore, Luke's Gospel must have been in circulation long enough before that time in order for both Paul and Timothy to know its contents and regard it as Scripture." *I Don't Have Enough Faith to Be an Atheist* (Wheaton, Illinois: Crossway, 2004), 241.

8. Paul Barnett, *Is the New Testament Reliable?* (Downers Grove, Illinois: IVP Academic, 2004), 99.

9. Legendary scholar William F. Albright, in *Recent Discoveries in Bible Lands*, claims that the New Testament was written no later than AD 80 (p. 136). John A. T. Robinson, one of the world's premier New Testament scholars and author of *Redating the New Testament*, placed John's gospel between AD 40 and sometime after AD 65.

10. Larry Stone, in his book *The Story of the Bible: The Fascinating History of Its Writing, Translation and Effect on Civilization*, writes: "Because Matthew, Mark, Luke, and John all tell the same story, numerous 'harmonies' of the gospels have been compiled in which the first three or all four gospels are put together in one narrative or compared side by side. The earliest harmony we know about is called the Diatessaron, a harmony of all four gospels, which was the work of Tatian, a pupil of Justin Martyr, between AD 150 and 160, fewer than one hundred years after the gospels were written. The Diatessaron, compiled in Syriac, is important because it was widely used instead of individual gospels in the Assyrian church for three hundred years. Greek and Old Latin versions of the Diatessaron were created a few years later." (Nashville, Tennessee: Thomas Nelson, 2013), 50–51.

11. Gary Habermas, *Evidence for The Historical Jesus: Is the Jesus of History the Christ of Faith?* (Cambridge, Ohio: Christian Publishing House, 2020), 22, Kindle.

12. Ibid.

13. The *Encyclopedia of the Bible* says this about the structure of 1 Timothy 3:16: "The balanced character of this passage suggests antiphonal usage. Similar in nature is 2 Timothy 2:11–13, which likewise suggests hymnic use. Another possible hymn fragment is Ephesians 5:14. The great Christological passage in Philippians 2:5–11 is clearly poetic in form and may reflect very early Christian hymnody." "New Testament Poetry," Bible Gateway, accessed October 24, 2022, https://www.biblegateway.com/resources/encyclopedia-of-the-bible/New-Testament-Poetry.

14. I emailed Dr. Gary Habermas to ask for a few sources that delve into the usage of the creed Paul recorded in 1 Timothy 3:16. He recommends Vernon Neufeld's *The Earliest Christian Confessions* and Richard Longenecker's *New Wine into Fresh Wineskins.*

15. Alister E. McGrath, *"I Believe": Exploring the Apostles' Creed* (Downers Grove, Illinois: InterVarsity Press, 1997), 104.

16. Irenaeus, *Against Heresies*, book 1, chapter 10, verse 1.

17. Ibid., book 5, chapter 3, verse 3.

18. Marcus J. Borg, *Meeting Jesus Again for the First Time: The Historical Jesus and the Heart of Contemporary Faith* (New York: HarperCollins, 1994), 17.

19. Marcus J. Borg, *Jesus: Uncovering the Life, Teachings, and Surprising Relevance of a Spiritual Revolutionary* (New York: HarperCollins, 2006), 198.

20. Bart D. Ehrman, *God's Problem: How the Bible Fails to Answer Our Most Important Question—Why We Suffer* (New York: HarperOne, 2008), 234.

21. Bart D. Ehrman, *Jesus Before the Gospels: How the Earliest Christians Remembered, Changed, and Invented Their Stories of the Savior* (New York: Harpercollins, 2016), 53.

22. Diarmaid MacCulloch, *A History of Christianity: The First Three Thousand Years* (London: Penguin Books, 2009), 94.

23. Norman L. Geisler and Jason Jimenez, *The Bible's Answers to 100 of Life's Biggest Questions* (Grand Rapids, Michigan: Baker Publishing Group, 2015), 81.

24. H. L. Willmington, *Willmington's Book of Bible Lists* (Wheaton, Illinois: Tyndale, 1987), 168–69.

25. "What Is Progressive Christianity?," Bethel Congregational United Church of Christ, accessed December 15, 2022, https://www.bethelbeaverton.org/progressive-christianity.

26. Richard Rohr, *The Universal Christ: How a Forgotten Reality Can Change Everything We See, Hope For, and Believe* (New York: Convergent, 2021), 171.

27. Ibid.

28. R. C. Symes, "The Resurrection Myths about Jesus: A Progressive Christian Interpretation," Investigating Philosophies, Culture, History, Myths, July 8, 2014, https://mbplee.wordpress.com/2014/07/08/the-resurrection-myths-about-jesus/.

29. Robert H. Gundry, *Soma in Biblical Theology: With Emphasis on Pauline Anthropology* (Cambridge: Cambridge University Press, 1976), 168.

30. Ibid., 169.

31. Charles C. Ryrie, *A Survey of Bible Doctrine* (Chicago: Moody Press, 1972), 75.

32. Ibid.

33. Wayne A. Grudem, *Systematic Theology: An Introduction to Biblical Doctrine* (Grand Rapids, Michigan: Zondervan, 1994), 609.

34. Ibid.

35. James Rowe Adams, "What Can Progressive Christians Say about Resurrection?," ProgressiveChristianity.org, July 25, 2006, https://progressivechristianity.org/resources/what-can-progressive-christians-say-about-resurrection.

36. Erwin W. Lutzer, *Christ among Other Gods: A Defense of Christ in an Age of Tolerance* (Chicago: Moody Publishers, 2016), 169.

Chapter 8: Hijacking Jesus's Second Coming

1. Pete Enns and Christopher Hays, "On Why Jesus Hasn't Come Back Yet (and the Answer May Shock You)," The Bible For Normal People, September 19, 2016, https://thebiblefornormalpeople.com/on-why-jesus-hasnt-come-back-yet/.
2. Robin R. Meyers, *Saving Jesus from the Church: How to Stop Worshiping Christ and Start Following Jesus* (New York: HarperCollins, 2010), 220.
3. John Dominic Crossan, *The Historical Jesus: The Life of a Mediterranean Jewish Peasant* (San Francisco: HarperCollins, 1991), 287–92.
4. Dale C. Allison, *The Historical Christ and the Theological Jesus* (Grand Rapids, Michigan: William B. Eerdmans Pub. Co., 2009), loc. 1197–1212, Kindle.
5. Ibid., 90.
6. Ibid.
7. Ibid., 91.
8. J. B. Lightfoot, trans., "The Epistle of Barnabas," Early Christian Writings, n.d., https://www.earlychristianwritings.com/text/barnabas-lightfoot.html.
9. Papias, *Fragments of Papias*, VI.
10. Irenaeus, *Against Heresies*, book 5, chapters 32–33.
11. The eminent historian Philip Schaff provides a solid summary of how prominently a literal rendering of Jesus's physical return to Earth figured in the early stages of Christianity: "The most striking point in the eschatology of the ante-Nicene age is the prominent chiliasm, or millenarianism, that is the belief of a visible reign of Christ in glory on earth with the risen saints for a thousand years, before the general resurrection and judgment. It was indeed not the doctrine of the church embodied in any creed or form of devotion, but a widely current opinion of distinguished teachers, such as Barnabas, Papias, Justin Martyr, Irenaeus, Tertullian, Methodius, and Lactantius; while Caius, Origen, Dionysius the Great, Eusebius (as afterwards Jerome and Augustine) opposed it. . . . It distinguishes, moreover, two resurrections, one before and another after the millennium, and makes the millennial reign of Christ only a prelude to his eternal reign in heaven, from which it is separated by a short interregnum of Satan. The millennium is expected to come not as the legitimate result of a historical process but as a sudden supernatural revelation. The advocates of this theory appeal to the certain promises of the Lord, but particularly to the hieroglyphic passage of the Apocalypse, which teaches a millennial reign of Christ upon this earth after the first resurrection and before the creation of the new heavens and the new earth. In connection with this the general expectation prevailed that the return of the Lord was near, though uncertain and unascertainable as to its day and hour, so that believers may be always ready for it. This hope, through the whole age of persecution, was a copious fountain of encouragement and comfort under the pains of that martyrdom which sowed in blood the seed of a bountiful harvest for the church." *History of the Christian Church* (Oak Harbor, Washington: Logos Research Systems, 1997), 2.XII.158.

12. George Eldon Ladd, *The Presence of the Future* (Grand Rapids, Michigan: Eerdmans, 1974), 4.

13. Enns and Hays, "On Why Jesus Hasn't Come Back Yet."

14. Marcus J. Borg, *Jesus: Uncovering the Life, Teachings, and Surprising Relevance of a Spiritual Revolutionary* (New York: HarperCollins, 2006), 258.

15. Crossan, *The Historical Jesus*, 287–92.

16. Meyers, *Saving Jesus from the Church*, 153–54.

17. Keith Giles, *Jesus Unexpected: Ending the End Times to Become the Second Coming* (Oak Glen, California: Quoir, 2020), 118–19.

18. Leading up to this event, Jesus had taught the Sermon on the Mount on the moral principles of the Kingdom of Heaven (Matthew 5–7), provided details of the present age (Matthew 13), and announced impending judgment on Judea (Matthew 21:41–44).

19. Tim LaHaye and Thomas Ice, *The End Times Controversy* (Eugene, Oregon: Harvest House, 2003), 378.

20. The phrase "times of the Gentiles" starts way back when Nebuchadnezzar conquered Jerusalem (586 BC) and Babylon came into power in 605 BC—resulting in the Jews going into captivity and not having full possession of their land as a people.

21. Michael J. Wilkins, *The NIV Application Commentary: Matthew* (Grand Rapids, Michigan: Zondervan Academic, 2004), 783.

22. Andrew Perriman, "Should We 'Water Down' the Doctrine of the Second Coming?," P.Ost, January 9, 2018, https://www.postost.net/2018/01/should-we -water-down-doctrine-second-coming.

23. This judgment is not to be confused with the Great White Throne Judgment (see Revelation 20:11–15), which will occur after the Millennial reign of Christ.

24. Here are a few other Bible passages about the Second Coming of Jesus: Isaiah 11:10–11; Jeremiah 23:5–6; Daniel 2:44–45; 7:9–14;12:1–3; Joel 2:1; Zechariah 12:10; 14:1–15; Matthew 13:41; 24:15–31; 26:64; Mark 13:14–27; 14:62; Luke 21:25–28; 3:19–21; 1 Thessalonians 3:13; 2 Thessalonians 1:6–10; 2:8; 1 Peter 4:12–13; 2 Peter 3:1–14; Jude 14–15; Revelation 1:7; 19:11–20:6; 22:7, 12.

25. Richard Rohr, *The Universal Christ: How a Forgotten Reality Can Change Everything We See, Hope For, and Believe* (New York: Convergent, 2021), 32.

26. David M. Felten and Jeff Procter-Murphy, *Living the Questions: The Wisdom of Progressive Christianity* (New York: HarperOne, 2012), 142.

27. Ibid., 138.

28. Barbara R. Rossing, *The Rapture Exposed: The Message of Hope in the Book of Revelation* (Boulder, Colorado: Westview Press, 2004), 134.

29. J. Dwight Pentecost, *Things to Come: A Study in Eschatology* (Grand Rapids, Michigan: Zondervan, 1958), 370.

30. Matt Carriker, "Excerpt from 'Giving Christianity Back to Jesus,'" ProgressiveChristianity.org, July 3, 2011, https://progressivechristianity.org /resources/excerpt-from-giving-christianity-back-to-jesus.

Chapter 9: Jesus, the Jewish Mystic

1. David A. Kaden, *Christianity in Blue: How the Bible, History, Philosophy, and Theology Shape Progressive Identity* (Minneapolis: Fortress Press, 2021), 81–82.
2. Marcus J. Borg, *Jesus: The Uncovering the Life, Teachings, and Surprising Relevance of a Spiritual Revolutionary* (New York: HarperCollins, 2006), 110.
3. Jeffrey Frantz, "Paul, a Jewish Christ Mystic," ProgressiveChristianity.org, August 6, 2021, https://progressivechristianity.org/resources/paul-a-jewish-christ-mystic.
4. However, Borg and Fredriksen would argue that the designated title "Son of God" given to Jesus in early Christianity did not carry divine qualities. They say it personified the content of His messages that made Jesus appear to possess divinity.
5. Marcus J. Borg, *Meeting Jesus Again for the First Time: The Historical Jesus and the Heart of Contemporary Faith* (New York: HarperCollins, 1994), 239–41.
6. John Shelby Spong, *Fourth Gospel: Tales of a Jewish Mystic* (New York: Harper Collins, 2013), 78.
7. Ibid., 86–87.
8. Adyashanti, *Resurrecting Jesus: Embodying the Spirit of a Revolutionary Mystic* (Boulder, Colorado: Sounds True, 2016), 34.
9. Ibid., foreword.
10. David G. Benner, *Spirituality and the Awakening Self: The Sacred Journey of Transformation* (Grand Rapids, Michigan: Baker Publishing Group, 2012), 76.
11. Barbara Karkabi, "Deepak Chopra Says Christ's Teachings Reach beyond the Christian Church," *Houston Chronicle*, March 8, 2008, https://www.chron.com/life/houston-belief/article/Deepak-Chopra-says-Christ-s-teachings-reach-1675413.php.
12. Peter Kreeft, "The Divinity of Christ," accessed November 5, 2022, https://peterkreeft.com/topics/christ-divinity.htm.
13. Craig Blomberg, *The Historical Reliability of the Gospels* (Downers Grove, Illinois: InverVarsity Press, 1987), 208.
14. Stephen Patterson and Marvin Meyer, trans., "The Gospel of Thomas," The Gnosis Archive, accessed November 5, 2022, http://www.gnosis.org/naghamm/gthpat.htm.

Chapter 10: Jesus, the Woke Teacher

1. Here is a statement posted on the GracePointe Church website: "The GracePointe community is leading the theological development and practice of Progressive Christianity. This is at the core of what makes us distinct and is far from a simple label change for a modern repackaging of traditional beliefs. . . . In 2015, GracePointe underwent a highly publicized process wherein it stated, publicly and absolutely, that LGBTQ+ people were welcomed, celebrated, and included at all levels of GracePointe's

community." "About Us," GracePointe Church, accessed April 6, 2023, https://www.gracepointe.net/about-us.

2.   *Merriam-Webster*, s.v. "woke (*adj.*)," accessed November 6, 2022, https://www.merriam-webster.com/dictionary/woke.

3.   In his book *Just Faith: Reclaiming Progressive Christianity*, Guthrie Graves-Fitzsimmons falsely aligns wokeness with the servant leadership taught by Jesus: "Progressive Christians don't want to be first for the sake of being first. We want to be first in line for the sake of the kingdom of heaven that's coming to earth. When we listen to Jesus speak about becoming a servant to all, that's a leadership style rather than a call to not assume any leadership. Servant leadership is humble, inclusive, and quick to confess errors along the way as we strive to improve our organizations and ourselves." (Minneapolis: Broadleaf Books, 2020), 168.

4.   Tony Campolo, "For the Record," The Positive Prophet of Red Letter Christianity, June 8, 2015, http://www.tonycampolo.org/for-the-record-tony-campolo-releases-a-new-statement/#.VXcdqc9Vikr.

5.   Richard Rohr and Mike Morrell, *The Divine Dance: The Trinity and Your Transformation* (New Kensington, Pennsylvania: Whitaker House, 2016), 137.

6.   Peter Wehner, "The Forgotten Radicalism of Jesus Christ," *New York Times*, December 24, 2020, https://www.nytimes.com/2020/12/24/opinion/jesus-christ-christmas-incarnation.html.

7.   Here are a few examples: (1) Jonathan Merritt, "The Politics of Jen Hatmaker: Trump, Black Lives Matter, Gay Marriage and More," Religion News Service, October 25, 2016, https://religionnews.com/2016/10/25/the-politics-of-jen-hatmaker-trump-black-lives-matter-gay-marriage-and-more; (2) John Pavlovitz, "6 Ways The Church's Treatment of LGBTQ People Is Actually Damaging the Church," *Stuff that Needs to Be Said* (blog), March 29, 2016, https://johnpavlovitz.com/2016/03/29/6-ways-churchs-treatment-lgbtq-people-actually-damaging-church; (3) Chris Seay's interview with Shane Claiborne in chapter four of his book *The Gospel According to Jesus: A Faith that Restores All Things*; (4) David P. Gushee, chapter seven, "Sex: From Sexual Purity to Covenant Realism," in his book *After Evangelicalism: The Path to a New Christianity*; (5) Jonathan Merritt's article on USA Today, "An Evangelical's Plea: 'Love the Sinner,'" https://usatoday30.usatoday.com/printedition/news/20090420/column20_st.art.htm; (6) Cathedral of Hope, "'UNCLOBBERING' – A Night with Colby Martin – PULSE – August 30, 2017," YouTube, August 30, 2017, https://youtu.be/CrQhWwnyaTI; (7) Guthrie Graves-Fitzsimmons, *Just Faith: Reclaiming Progressive Christianity*; (8) Rob Bell, interview with Odyssey Networks, https://youtu.be/-q0iDaW6BnE.

8.   Daniel David Joseph, "If Jesus Were Alive Today . . ." ProgressiveChristianity.org, March 5, 2021, https://progressivechristianity.org/resources/if-jesus-were-alive-today.

9.   David P. Gushee, in *After Evangelicalism: The Path to a New Christianity* (Louisville, Kentucky: Westminster John Knox Press, 2020), 65, 88.

10. A reoccurring theme I found in most progressive Christian books is how they victimize themselves and mischaracterize biblical Christianity. Here's a small taste from Guthrie Graves-Fitzsimmons, *Just Faith: Reclaiming Progressive Christianity* (Minneapolis: Broadleaf Books, 2020), 22: "Even as progressives lay claim to a bold tradition that sides with the vulnerable and decries oppressive systems, in our American context today, conservative Christians portray themselves as the 'traditional Christians' who resist any changes to their claimed tradition—whether it's scientific understanding of the world, LGBTQ rights, or the countries growing non-white population. Progress and change are pitted against tradition by many conservative Christians. That's not surprising. Progressives have not always been met with acceptance or welcome from the official church structures. But then again, official religious institutions didn't get too high a grade from Jesus."

11. Diana Butler Bass, *Freeing Jesus: Rediscovering Jesus as Friend, Teacher, Savior, Lord, Way, and Presence* (San Francisco: HarperOne, 2021), 261.

12. Greg Koukl, "The Legend of the Social Justice Jesus," Stand to Reason, November 1, 2021, https://www.str.org/w/the-legend-of-the-social-justice-jesus.

13. Rachel Held Evans, "LGBTQ+," *Rachel Held Evans* (blog), October 8, 2019, rachelheldevans.com/blog/lgbtq; Jen Hatmaker's podcast episode, "A Call to Openness & Affirmation: A Panel Discussion With LGBTQ+ Faith Leaders"; Rob Bell's debate with Andrew Wilson, "Homosexuality and the Bible," YouTube, https://youtu.be/XF9uo_P0nNI; Derek Webb's song "What Matters More"; Brian McLaren, *A New Kind of Christianity*; Brandan Robertson debate with Jeff Durbin and James White, https://youtu.be/ti0FzdOHW_8.

14. Chris Kratzer, *Stupid Sh*t Heard in Church* (United States: self-pub., 2021), 56.

15. Whitney Hopler, "Your Identity in Christ—14 Things God Says of You List," Crosswalk.com, January 14, 2013, https://www.crosswalk.com/faith/spiritual-life/how-to-find-your-true-identity-in-christ.html.

16. Peter J. Gomes, *The Good Book: Reading the Bible with Mind and Heart* (New York: HarperOne, 2002), 208.

17. Anthony C. Thiselton, *The First Epistle to the Corinthians: A Commentary on the Greek Text* (Grand Rapids, Michigan: William B. Eerdmans Pub. Co., 2013), 452.

18. Rosaria Butterfield, "Love Your Neighbor Enough to Speak Truth," The Gospel Coalition, October 31, 2016, https://www.thegospelcoalition.org/article/love-your-neighbor-enough-to-speak-truth.

19. Erwin W. Lutzer, *Christ among Other Gods: A Defense of Christ in an Age of Tolerance* (Chicago: Moody Publishers, 2016), 65–66.

Chapter 11: Jesus, the Revolutionist

1. R. David Kaylor, *Jesus the Prophet: His Vision of the Kingdom on Earth* (Louisville, Kentucky: Westminster/John Knox Press, 1994), 3.

2. Brad R. Braxton, "Getting in Front of Jesus: The Politics of Progressive Christianity (Part I)," HuffPost, updated May 25, 2011, https://www.huffpost.com/entry/getting-in-front-of-jesus_b_649152.

3. Ibid.

4. Jonathan Merritt, "Theologian Says Jesus Was a 'Trickster'—but It's Not as Offensive as You Think," Religion News Service, January 28, 2015, https://religionnews.com/2015/01/28/theologian-says-jesus-trickster-not-offensive-think.

5. Dawn Hutchings, "Time to Vaccinate Ourselves against the Infection of Atonement Theology," ProgressiveChristianity.org, April 2, 2021, https://progressivechristianity.org/resources/time-to-vaccinate-ourselves-against-the-infection-of-atonement-theology.

6. John Dominic Crossan, *Jesus: A Revolutionary Biography* (San Francisco: Harper, 1994), 300.

7. N. T. Wright, *Jesus and the Victory of God*, vol. 2 (Minneapolis: Fortress Press, 1996), 92.

8. Ibid.

9. Braxton, "Getting in Front of Jesus: The Politics of Progressive Christianity (Part I)."

10. Benjamin Cain, "The Clash of Progressive and Evangelical Christianities," Medium, January 26, 2021, https://medium.com/interfaith-now/the-clash-between-progressive-and-evangelical-christianity-dcbb6f6f72d2.

11. Brian Zahnd, *The Unvarnished Jesus* (self-pub., 2019), 26–28.

12. Brian Zahnd, (@BrianZahnd), "What some call social justice Jesus called the kingdom of God," Twitter, September 6, 2018, 10:20 a.m., https://twitter.com/brianzahnd/status/1037707100753985537.

13. John Pavlovitz, "Progressive Christianity—Is Christianity," *Stuff That Needs to Be Said* (blog), October 5, 2016, https://johnpavlovitz.com/2016/10/05/explaining-progressive-christianity-otherwise-known-as-christianity.

14. Cain, "The Clash of Progressive and Evangelical Christianities."

15. Jen Hatmaker, *Interrupted: When Jesus Wrecks Your Comfortable Christianity* (Colorado Springs: NavPress, 2014), 30.

16. Greg Koukl, "The Legend of the Social Justice Jesus," Stand to Reason, November 1, 2021, https://www.str.org/w/the-legend-of-the-social-justice-jesus.

17. Lawrence W. Reed, "Rendering unto Caesar: Was Jesus a Socialist?," Foundation for Economic Education, March 3, 2015, https://fee.org/resources/rendering-unto-caesar-was-jesus-a-socialist.